Why We
LOVE
the Way
WE DO

Also by Preeti Shenoy

The Secret Wish List

The One You Cannot Have

It Happens for a Reason

It's All in the Planets

A Hundred Little Flames

The Rule Breakers

The Magic Mindset: How to Find Your Happy Place

A Place Called Home

The Homecoming

Why We LOVE the Way WE DO

PREETI SHENOY

HARPER NON-FICTION

First published in 2015
This edition published in India by Harper Non-Fiction 2025
An imprint of HarperCollins *Publishers*
4th Floor, Tower A, Building No. 10, DLF Cyber City, DLF Phase II,
Gurugram, Haryana – 122002
www.harpercollins.co.in

2 4 6 8 10 9 7 5 3 1

Copyright © Preeti Shenoy 2015, 2025

P-ISBN: 978-93-5629-289-5
E-ISBN: 978-93-5629-297-0

The views and opinions expressed in this book are the author's own and the facts are as reported by her, and the publishers are not in any way liable for the same.

This book discusses themes of love, heartbreak and coping, including mentions of self-harm and harmful actions. The content of this book should not replace consultation with your doctor or qualified mental health specialists for anyone experiencing anxiety, depression, suicidal ideation, or any other emotional or mental health concerns. The author and the publisher disclaim any liability or responsibility to any person or entity for any loss, damage, injury, or expense that may arise from the use of any content in this book. Any use of, or reliance on, information in this book is solely the responsibility of the reader.

Preeti Shenoy asserts the moral right
to be identified as the author of this work.

All rights reserved. No part of this publication may be reproduced, stored in a retrieval system, or transmitted, in any form or by any means, electronic, mechanical, photocopying, recording or otherwise, without the prior permission of the publishers.

Typeset in 11.5/14 Usherwood Std
HarperCollins *Publishers* India

Printed and bound at
Manipal Technologies Limited, Manipal

This book is produced from independently certified FSC® paper to ensure responsible forest management.

For Satish, Atul and Purvi
And for Anukul, Vani and Manu too

Contents

Introduction   *xi*

FINDING THE ONE   **1**
1. Why we cannot help whom we fall in love with   3
2. Finding love in a virtual world   7
3. Playing hard to get   12
4. How jealousy ruins relationships   16
5. Kisses—the lifeblood of a relationship   22
6. Finding and keeping love online and long-distance relationships   25
7. How Tinder changed Valentine   30
8. What to do when you are friend-zoned   34
9. How to tell if it is love or lust   39
10. How music affects love   43
11. On making a relationship last through the years   47
12. Is our love for someone immortal?   52

GETTING HITCHED   **57**
13. Why proposals are always on bended knees   59
14. Finding the right person to marry   63
15. How to tell if someone is too old or too young for you   70
16. Does marriage take away your freedom?   77

17. The three-year itch in marriages	82
18. How to handle fights in a relationship	85
19. Can senior citizens find love?	89

WHEN THINGS GO WRONG — 95
20. Why break-ups hurt so much — 97
21. How to deal with a broken heart — 102
22. How heartbreaks can take lives — 110
23. How moving homes is like breaking up — 114

ON MEN AND WOMEN — 119
24. Why women love high heels — 121
25. Is casual sex worth the effort? — 125
26. Is friends-with-benefits a good option in relationships? — 133
27. Why watches are male and keys are female — 137
28. Why flirting is good for you — 141
29. How cuddling helps a relationship — 144
30. What makes you a bad girl in India? — 147
31. Why space is important in a relationship — 150

LET'S TALK — 155
32. Why the written word is a catalyst for love — 157
33. How nagging affects a relationship — 161
34. How anger affects relationships — 165
35. Why we talk the way we do — 169
36. Why laughter is important in a relationship — 176
37. Why respect is important in a relationship — 180
38. How expectations twist a relationship — 185
39. Why it is important to express what you feel — 189
40. How often should you message a person you fancy? — 193
41. How to communicate when there is a conflict — 197

Contents

THREE TO TANGO **203**
42. How extramarital affairs start 205
43. How to maintain balance in a relationship 209
44. Can finger length predict a propensity to cheat? 213
45. Are we genetically programmed to stray? 216
46. Affairs in the workplace 223

BETWEEN THE SHEETS **227**
47. Would you sleep with someone for money? 229
48. Do women really want muscular men? 232
49. Sex and the Indian woman 235
50. What your sleeping position says about your relationship 238
51. How important is sex in a relationship? 242
52. What does consent mean when it comes to sex? 245
53. What's your dirtiest fantasy? 248
54. Sex and the Indian teen 251
55. What turns you on? 254
56. How erotica differs from porn 257

Acknowledgements *261*

Introduction

A QUESTION I AM often asked is, 'When was it that you decided that you wanted to be a writer?' My answer to that one never varies. There really wasn't an exact defining moment. I have written ever since I learnt how to. My affair with the written word continued well into my college years and I wrote many short stories, some of which won prizes at the university level. But I never thought that I would actually become a novelist—or would be writing my own column in a national newspaper.

This book is a collection of pieces adapted from my column 'Sex and the City', written over the last one-and-a-half years for the *Financial Chronicle*. I thoroughly enjoyed the writing experience, as the column is on relationships, sex, communication between men and women, finding the perfect partner and anything else that you can think of on those lines. The inspiration for these columns comes from real life stories that many people have shared with me over the years. People seem to consider me a 'relationship expert'. I get mails from complete strangers who share with me the most intimate details of their lives and ask me for my advice. Now here is the thing—when I am not directly involved in something, the perspective I have from my vantage point is so different from the one someone badly entangled in the situation has. So whenever I have offered my thoughts, they have always been graciously received. Through the stories that people shared with me, what I discovered was that when it comes to relationships and love, we are all slaves of our heart, whether we are in our forties or our twenties.

Surprisingly most people are okay when I ask them if I can write about what they have told me. In fact, they urge me to do so as they feel it will help others in a similar situation. So in many places in this book I have shared real stories, but I have changed the details and the names to protect identities.

Most of what I have said in the book comes from a combination of many hours of research and many years of experience. While writing the columns, I had to be certain what I was saying was backed by scientific research and studies. So I investigated and read up. I was intrigued by some of the things I discovered. Some of it confirmed what I already knew. Some of it came as a surprise. I also learnt about many things: for example, how the dynamics of a relationship works, whether there is a pattern, whether we can control things like choosing whom we fall in love with, what we can do to make the relationship last, how we can tell if it is love or lust, and so on. I have shared it all in this book.

The book is divided into seven sections. *Finding the One* is largely about finding love and deals with the dating stage; *Getting Hitched* is about marriage; *When Things Go Wrong* deals with break-ups and all things associated; *On Men and Women* focuses on gender differences; *Let's Talk* deals with how differently men and women communicate; *Three to Tango* is about infidelity; and *Between the Sheets* is about sex. You can read them in any order you like—that is the beauty of a collection like this one.

Thank you very much for reading this book and I sincerely hope you enjoy it, find it useful and, most importantly, I hope it makes you think.

Preeti Shenoy
August 2015

FINDING THE ONE

Life without love is like a tree without blossoms or fruit.

–Kahlil Gibran

Why we cannot help whom we fall in love with

SOMEONE I KNOW IS a self-confessed love-addict. He is thirty-two, works at a mid-management level in a corporate organisation and is doing really well in his career. It is just that he doesn't seem to have found The One, and he flits from one relationship to the next.

'I can't help it. It is the thrill of that initial, giddy, out-of-control feeling that happens in every new relationship that I am addicted to,' he admits.

He has been in seven wildly unsuitable relationships so far. And each one ended in a disaster. It wasn't that he did not love the women. It was just that he found a reason to break off each time.

'What happens when you get to know her better? Why don't you make an effort to see it through?' I prod.

'Too much work, really. And once I get to know a woman better, the mystery vanishes.'

'So does she just become another notch on your bedpost? Do you even realise how that makes you sound?' I ask in mock-horror. Of course I know him very well and I am only teasing him. It is just that he is too much of an idealist and is still seeking the 'perfect woman'. But I am not going to tell him so and lose an opportunity to rile him a little.

'Yes, I am aware. I am a serial philanderer and I am never going to get married,' he says with a straight face.

'I would like to see you falling in love. I mean true love. You will be singing a different tune then.'

'I too am waiting for that day,' he sighs.

If we are to go by what the movies and novels tell us, falling in love just happens. If it is a Hindi movie, you hear a melodious track in the background, the lyrics usually waxing eloquent about the heroine's beauty, comparing various parts of her anatomy to the moon, stars, the sun—even Fevicol. This is accompanied by the hero gazing at her with the expression of a glutton discovering a six-course banquet consisting of various gastronomical delights.

In real life though, falling in love often happens over a period of time. You see someone gorgeous and get attracted strongly. If you strike up a conversation, find each other likable—or intriguing, as the case may be—then you exchange phone numbers or email ids. After a couple of dates, discovering many things and maybe a kiss or something more, depending on how much in resonance your moral compasses are, the magic happens, and *wham*, you are in love.

This seems to suggest that we have no control over whom we fall for; that it is just destined to happen. But science has discovered otherwise. When we feel attracted to someone, our brains actually perform a series of complex calculations in a matter of a few seconds. All the five senses are involved in making these calculations and it all happens subconsciously. The eyes are the first to react. That explains why we are drawn to good looks, long, lustrous hair—a symbol of fertility—and a clear complexion, indicating a good reproductive fitness level, which we are genetically programmed to seek to propagate the species. Once we move closer, the nose comes into play. We are not just attracted to that irresistible deo he has used—despite what the ads portray—but we are drawn to pheromones which are naturally produced by our bodies.

In a study, ovulating women were each asked to wear the same T-shirt for three nights. Male volunteers were then asked to smell the T-shirts along with some fresh ones. The testosterone levels shot up when they sniffed the ones that had been worn, as against the fresh ones. In a similar experiment, women were asked to smell T-shirts worn by men, and were asked to pick the ones whose smell appealed to them. It was discovered that they had a natural propensity to pick out those men whose genes differed greatly from theirs. We are wired to mate with men whose genes will give offspring a survival advantage.

Once the sight and smell gets out of the way, we then focus on the voice. It was found that men prefer women with a high-pitched breathy voice, which suggests a smaller body size, and women are drawn to men with deeper voices, indicating a larger body size. The final test of whether a budding relationship will bloom or wilt is the first kiss. This is so, as kissing involves a lot of tactile information exchange. When we kiss someone, we discover the taste of their mouth and the smell of their breath. Science tells us that this is a huge factor in determining attraction. A majority of men and women have reported losing the attraction if the first kiss was bad or if their olfactory bulbs did not light up and instead went kaput, much like the unpredictable power-cuts that happen across our country.

If the physical chemistry between two people is great, then our bodies release something called norepinephrine, which usually activates our fight or flight senses, and our hearts begin to beat to the rhythm of the lungi dance in *Chennai Express*. Without our realising it, our pupils dilate and our bodies release glucose—not because there is a signal of danger, but because it senses that something important is happening.

The initial attraction thus is a biological drive and not just happenstance. After the couple has been together for a few years, the relationship evolves into different levels like true love and unconditional love.

Sexual attraction and compatibility are two completely different things though. You might be crazily drawn to a certain person, but discover that you have nothing to say to him or her. You might be able to talk the whole night with certain other people, but when you meet, there may be no spark to light a fire, which is probably the case with most relationships that my friend has had so far.

If you are in luck and get both, attraction as well as compatibility, in a single person as a package deal, manage to grab it before the light goes out and make it permanent by marriage, then you spend the rest of your life trying to suppress your norepinephrine, telling it with earnestness: 'No, don't react please. I am married now.'

But, just like a teenager, it will listen to you only when it wants to.

Finding love in a virtual world

DIVYA, A YOUNG GIRL in her mid-twenties who is doing an MBA, was visiting me and she kept checking her phone.

'Expecting a message from you-know-who,' she confessed, her face alight. Just then the phone buzzed. She smiled as she read the text on the screen. 'Excuse me for a second,' she said as she deftly tapped out a reply and then we resumed our conversation.

Anyone who has been in the early stages of love will know how Divya felt at that moment. We live in a world where we can connect with anyone via our phones and 140-character messages. Nobody, not even the prime minister of the country or the hottest Bollywood or Hollywood celebrity, is off-limits. Unhappy about something? Out comes the phone and you tap away expressing yourself, telling people how you feel. There are no filters here. A thought enters your head and within seconds the whole world—or at least the people who follow you on social media—is privy to it.

In the times we live in, the style of courtship and getting into a relationship with that special person has changed too. Most of us strive to get that unique connection which will transport us to a magical place where nothing matters but being with that special person. The movies and the books tell us that it is indeed possible, as do the photos of happy couples that pop up all over your feed as soon as the relationship status changes from 'single' to 'committed'. But there are subtle things to bear in mind here too as we navigate the path of true love, wielding our smartphones and sending out messages to potential mates.

Everyone knows that a wink typed at the end of a message isn't just a wink. It is a complex code signalling anything from 'I might not mean that' to 'I am horny'.

As though trying to decipher the intentions of the other sex wasn't hard enough without the interference of technology, the dating-mating scene today has taken on forms which even Jan Koum (or Neeraj Arora, if you want to be patriotic) would not have foreseen, with unwritten rules being changed faster than hashtags at the end of a tweet.

When WhatsApp had an outage for about two hours shortly after being bought by Facebook, the whole internet went berserk with unabashed declarations such as 'I didn't block you, darling, whatsapp is down' popping up as status messages even on profiles of people who weren't twenty-somethings with relationship statuses reading 'It's complicated'.

In an age where technology has integrated seamlessly into every aspect of our life, including romance and the way we connect with each other, calling up someone, which a couple of years ago would have been normal if a guy wanted to ask a girl out, would today be considered being too pushy. You don't call, you ping.

And there are rules for pinging too, depending on the length of time you have known the person. If you do not know them at all, you first stalk them on Facebook, studying their life through DPs (display pictures for the uninitiated) posted over the years, movies liked, books read (or not read) and the kind of music that makes them tick (or makes you want to run in the opposite direction; oh wait—shouldn't it be 'log out'?). You then 'approach' them by casually 'liking' a public post they made. Do not make the mistake of commenting yet, as you might be seen as being 'too forward'. And horror of horrors, if you have 'liked' something that they posted more than three years ago, your online stalking would be exposed and you can be certain you will be relegated to the 'creep category', blocked and ignored, even before you have had a chance to say a virtual hi. So take your time and check the date of the posting before hitting 'like'.

Now you wait for them to 'like' one of your posts. Waiting for that 'like' has replaced the earlier 'waiting for the phone to ring'. Once the initial hesitant, carefully-chosen 'likes' are exchanged with a potential partner, depending on how fast you want the relationship to move, you like some more pictures, status messages or comments. Only when this ritual is cleared do you proceed to the next step, which is to drop a message. (Note, it's only a message, not an email.) If the other person isn't on your friend list yet, there is a waiting period for that too, as it lands in the 'other' folder. If the person is equally interested in you and hence scans the 'other' folder, reads your carefully constructed message positioned to sound casual-yet-interested and replies (hooray!), it is a clear signal for you to send a friend request. If accepted, do not rejoice yet, for this is merely a virtual foot in the virtual door of a *very* complicated virtual relationship that may or may not flourish.

Presuming that all the above parameters are tick-marked with the precision of a math teacher grading a particularly hard test-paper, you meet for a first date. You rack your brains as to what to talk about, as you already know the music they like, the books they read (or didn't) and the movies they watched. What earlier was 'ice-breaking small talk' on a first date will now expose you as an ignoramus who doesn't know how to use social media or isn't tech-savvy if you ask the usual 'let's get to know each other better' kind of questions, the kind that people *used* to ask on a first date. A better bet would be to say, 'Oh, it feels like I already know you so well,' which would not be far from the truth, if you have done your homework, of studying the DPs, likes and comments.

After this first date comes the wait. Oh, the agony of a wait for a reply to a ping! If you want to torture a person, a guaranteed way would be to not answer their pings for at least a day. This was what Divya had been experiencing till the reply arrived.

If the person still holds your interest after twenty-four hours, congratulations—you have just accomplished a mammoth leap towards defeating the virtual world, with a baby step into a real relationship.

But if the ping doesn't come, never mind. There are more than fifty major social networking sites waiting to ask you 'what's on your mind'.

Playing hard to get

WHEN YOU ARE SINGLE and trying to get that cute guy or that stunning woman at the bar, your workplace, the library or local gym to notice you, it can be very confusing to decipher if he or she is truly not interested in you or is just playing hard to get.

Arpit and Dipali experienced this first hand. Arpit was in his third year of B.Com, and Dipali was a year junior to him. Dipali stayed in the hostel while Arpit lived with his parents. They had plenty of opportunities to interact with each other as both were members of their college Commerce Association. They got talking and found they had many things in common and that they genuinely enjoyed each other's company. Arpit asked Dipali out and while she wanted to instantly accept, as she was delighted, her closest friend Vaidehi advised her against it. She said if she accepted too easily, Arpit wouldn't value her. Though it wasn't what Dipali wanted to do, she decided to take Vaidehi's advice and turned him down with an excuse.

Arpit asked her out again the following week and this time she had to attend a family function in her home town and couldn't accept. By the third week she was desperate to go on a date with him and told him that, come what may, they would go out that weekend for a movie. This time it was Arpit who turned her down! He said that he had already made plans with another girl who had asked him out. Dipali felt really bad about it and wished that she had accepted the first time he'd asked. Their relationship never got a chance to develop. Vaidehi maintains that if he was interested enough, he would have waited and asked her again, but Dipali feels that she unnecessarily complicated something when there was no need for it.

The thing about playing hard to get is that it is a double-edged sword and you have to be a master of the game to be able to use it to your advantage. One wrong move and it can slip, slicing the relationship and your heart (or theirs) in the process, killing what could have been wonderful before it even had a chance to blossom.

There are many people who put honesty above mind-games and have ended relationships as the stress of figuring out where they stand in somebody's life, especially when they have been left guessing a tad too many times, gets impossible to endure. Then again there are others for whom the chase is the elixir their attraction thrives on. They do not want somebody who is predictable, always there and willing to go out with them at last-minute notice on a Saturday night.

According to researchers Dai, Dong and Jia, whose paper has been published in the journal of US National Library and National Institute of Health, playing hard to get works only under certain circumstances: i.e., where the partners are already interested in each other and emotionally invested to a certain degree in the relationship. If one of the parties is not interested, playing hard to get will not motivate the other person to chase. Thus, this strategy has a chance of working only if a potential partner already knows and likes you. This was why Arpit and Dipali's relationship never took off.

The thing is—each of us are complex individuals with our own quirks, likes and dislikes, not to mention mood-swings, stress and a hundred other factors that affect the decisions that we make daily. When it comes to playing hard to get, no matter what the research says, one person's turn-on might be another person's passion-killer. Personally, if somebody was sending me 'stay away from me' signals, I would take that at face value and do just that. And if I was interested in someone, I wouldn't play mind-games thinking that it would increase their desire for me. I would instead make it known that they matter and would ask them out and see if I liked their company. And if they didn't return my calls after a couple of attempts, I definitely would not 'chase them' as it instantly conjures up an image of a cowboy with a lasso, trying to loop in something that is attempting to get away. A relationship has to glide effortlessly, more so in the early stages.

While there is a whole load of information out there that tells men how to make her beg for sex with tips like more foreplay, waiting for the right moment, giving her a teaser of the things to come—kissing her softly and tenderly, pressing her against the wall and looking into her eyes, and so on—what they forget to tell you is that most women like guys who are genuinely sweet and sincere. Every woman loves a guy who will listen to her, converse intelligently with her, treat her with respect, admire her mind more than her body and, most importantly, a guy who keeps his word. Thus, if you have promised someone that you will call her on Wednesday, put a reminder on your phone and make that call. If you have told her that you will get back to her on something, ensure you do so by the promised time. Little things like these are what would make a woman impressed with a man. No woman likes to be kept on tenterhooks wondering where she stands with a guy.

My male friends tell me that it is the same for men. Most guys would hate a woman who doesn't keep her promises, who treats them like her personal errand boy and does not respect them.

The rules of a relationship are simple. If you like them, let them know. If they say no, let them go.

Now, that isn't so hard to get, is it?

How jealousy ruins relationships

WHEN MY DAUGHTER WAS a baby, she would never let me talk to anyone. If I as much as attempted a conversation with someone when she was in my arms, she would make loud noises, hold my face and turn it towards her, demanding my complete attention. Now my children are all grown up and there are no such displays of jealousy, but the mantle seems to have been taken over by my dog! When I hug my spouse, my dog feels jealous. She whines, makes a fuss and demands to be petted. And she continues to do so till I give her some attention. Animals and children never hide their feelings. What they feel is what you see. It is we adults who are more complicated to unravel than tangled Christmas fairy lights. Yet some basic factors never change.

While in school and college, the usual trick a boy used to get the attention of a girl he was interested in was to ignore her completely and talk to her best friend. It was a guaranteed way to annoy her and get her to pay him some attention. If you are in school or college, you will be familiar with this ploy. And if you are in a relationship, then too you will be familiar

How jealousy ruins relationships

with it, as couples who have been together for a while sometimes use the 'jealousy' gambit to get their negligent partner to pay some attention to them: they flirt with a member of the opposite sex in the hope that the partner notices.

Most of us who have been in relationships have experienced jealousy in varying degrees at some point or the other. Jealousy, that little voice in our head constantly chiming a chant of 'hey, watch out for that attractive person out to steal your mate', is often controlled, subdued, suppressed or asked to take a hike. We battle it with logic—after all, your spouse or partner has always been faithful and has never given you a reason to doubt his/her motives—and deal with it by not allowing it to grow.

But at times it can take gargantuan proportions like the mythical Greek Empusa who ensnared unsuspecting victims with her charm and then devoured them. It can overwhelm and wreak havoc in a relationship. The very thing which in small quantities binds two people together—for a little bit of jealousy shows that you care about that other person an awful lot—can drive them apart so far that it becomes impossible to bridge the gap.

For instance, take the case of Daivik and Rachna. They had been in a relationship for five years. It had stemmed from their college days, where both had studied together. Daivik is an extremely attractive guy, and Rachna always felt he was out of her league. While they were in college, she would sometimes feel jealous of the attention he got from girls, but since she was always around him, she was able to 'keep an eye' on him. He didn't mind and found it 'cute' that she was possessive about him. When they started working they joined different organisations, and it was here that Rachna's jealousy grew out of control. She started obsessing about the women Daivik would deal with while at work. When they met, she would question him at length. Initially he humoured her, but soon started getting annoyed with her behaviour. They started having many fights over this. The last straw for Daivik came when Rachna insisted on checking his phone to see who he had been chatting with. To Daivik, it was her mistrust that broke his heart, especially as he had never been unfaithful to her. Rachna says that though she knew she was being paranoid, she just couldn't stop herself. It was like she was caught in the grip of compulsive behaviour from which she could not escape. She felt bad when she questioned Daivik, but she felt worse when she did not confront him and tried to supress her suspicions. And thus whenever they met, the same scenario would repeat itself. Finally Daivik decided to break up with Rachna. He said he had been changing as a person because of her behaviour. He was naturally an extrovert and a fun-loving person, but because of her possessiveness and accusations, he had started becoming more guarded and less sociable. He hated how he was changing and wanted to just be himself.

The theme of jealousy has been dealt with in many movies, the most memorable one for me being *Vicky Cristina Barcelona,* in which two women who are friends fall in love with the same guy, unaware that his ex-wife—for whom he still has feelings—is about to enter the picture. The jealousy is depicted powerfully, where the ex-wife just cannot stay away from him, and he too pines and craves for her, despite having broken up.

In the 2006 Bollywood movie *Omkara,* an adaptation of Shakespeare's *Othello,* Omi smothers his new wife to death because he suspects her of having an affair with another man, only to repent later as he realises what a terrible misunderstanding it was.

Jealousy also forms the theme for many well-known works of literature as well as art. Agnolo Bronzino's 'Venus, Cupid, Folly and Time', painted in 1545, which hangs in the National Gallery in London, shows a nude Venus with Cupid kissing her, his hand on her breast, as Father Time, depicted by an old man, watches on. A dark figure howling in agony just behind them is Jealousy.

Edward Munch, who incidentally happens to be one of my favourite artists, painted 'Jealousy' in 1895. The painting depicts a man and a woman in the background, the woman standing with her robe open to reveal her nakedness as she reaches for an apple—a reference to the temptation of Adam by Eve. The face of the man she is with is not revealed. The woman is said to be Dagny Juel, with whom Munch had a relationship. Depicted in the foreground of the painting is Juel's husband, the Polish poet Stanislaw Przybyszewski. His jealousy is evident from the expression on his face. Thus jealousy, the biblical allegory of temptation, and Munch's love for Dagny converge in this poignant work of art.

In literature, the famous handkerchief in *Othello* bears testimony to the destructive power of jealousy. In Marcel Proust's *Remembrance of Things Past*, Swann sits at home, just after having left Odette. Suddenly it occurs to him that she might have gone to meet somebody. In a jealous fit he takes a cab and goes to where she lives. The entire street is dark and he sees a light trickling out beneath a door only in her house. He tiptoes up and stands outside her house and peeps in—only to discover two old men. It is the wrong house. Jealousy has blinded him so much that he is tortured and pained.

In another wonderful book *The Unbearable Lightness of Being* by Milan Kundera, Terez, who is married to Tomas, is driven by jealousy to befriend Tomas's lover, Sabina. Even though it is a terrible thing for her to endure, she carries the burden as she is so consumed by this dark emotion and is in its manic grip, unable to break free. Literature thus bears testimony to this powerful emotion that can change lives forever.

Jealousy can be of two kinds—normal or delusional. And the thing with jealousy is that it is so grey and so very powerful that it is often indistinguishable as to which one it is. An example would be a man who is perfectly reasonable in all aspects of his life, but insanely jealous when it comes to his faithful, loving and good-looking wife. He spies on her phone calls, keeps tabs on the people she meets, does not want her to have associations with anybody other than himself, and thinks that she is lying to him, despite her repeatedly proving her fidelity. A jealous wife may throw a fit over a husband or a partner taking a female colleague out for coffee and may make his life miserable in the many ways that only a jealous spouse can, like it happened in the case of Daivik and Rachna.

Jealousy can be very detrimental to a relationship, sucking out the love and slowly replacing it with venom. If it rears its ugly head, it is important to fight it and kill it. However, sometimes the monster, despite efforts to extinguish it, wins and anyone who has experienced intense jealousy knows that it can drive a person to a place beyond logic, a place where emotions run uncontrolled and a person who is otherwise loving turns into a bully on a destruction spree, making accusations, hurling verbal abuse and saying things in the heat of the moment that strike the very soul.

And while a relationship might ultimately survive this rampage, it would forever be laden with its scars.

Kisses—the lifeblood of a relationship

A KISS ON THE lips has always been a subject guaranteed to quicken pulse rates and hold anybody's interest. This ultimate symbol of passion and romance has been depicted for many centuries now in several celebrated works of art, each one an image of an unforgettable love story.

Francesca da Rimini was an Italian aristocrat who lived in the thirteenth century. She fell in love with her husband's brother Paulo, and they managed to carry on an affair for about ten years till her husband walked in on them in bed. He instantly killed them both. Dante later used her as a character in one of his works, *The Inferno*. The story of Francesca and Paulo has inspired several theatrical and symphonic adaptations, poems and many artworks including Auguste Rodin's most famous sculpture, 'The Kiss', where the lips of the lovers never actually touch, denoting the tragic end to the love story.

In Ovid's *Metamorphoses*, a sculptor envisions the ideal woman and she is brought to life by Goddess Venus. Overjoyed, hardly believing his luck, swept by passion, he kisses her on the lips. The New York

Metropolitan Museum houses the artwork inspired by the story—'Pygmalion and Galatea', painted by Jean-Leon Gerome in 1890.

'The Kiss' by Gustav Klimt, which is one of my favourite works of art, is an erotic masterpiece that depicts a couple in a tight embrace, the man bending down to plant a kiss on the welcoming cheek of a lover, shown with eyes closed, a close-lipped smile and a look of pure rapture. If ever put up for sale, it is likely to be the most expensive piece of art in history, as Klimt's earlier work sold for a record 135 million US dollars.

Sometime back, a short film by Tatia Pilieva went viral, gathering more than seventy million views on YouTube, the number burgeoning every day. It was purportedly a candid recording of twenty people, complete strangers to each other, being asked to indulge in an intimate kiss on the lips for the camera. They are awkward and shy at first, and then turn very intimate, the chemistry sizzling. It turned out that the film was actually an advertisement for a new clothing line, and the 'strangers' were in fact models, actors and musicians. Most people who were initially floored by its candidness—for they believed it was a slice of real life magic—felt duped to discover it was just an advertisement, and they poured out their disappointment on Twitter and Facebook.

In the 2014 Bollywood movie *Queen*, a kiss on the lips with a sexy Italian chef becomes the ultimate symbol of liberation for a middle-class Indian girl, raised with 'proper Indian values' and 'proper Indian culture'. She leaps gleefully, having broken a taboo, and leaves him, even though she has a chance to pursue a relationship with him if she wants.

However, among all the kisses immortalised, whether through paintings, sculptures, movies or the internet, my personal number one favourite remains Rene Magritte's painting 'The Lovers', which shows a man and a woman kissing. What is unusual is that the heads of both are covered completely in grey fabric. On first glance the painting may look absurd and surreal, but with a little reflection, it can be interpreted in many ways. Perhaps it is a relationship shrouded in secrecy because of societal norms, or maybe it illustrates that all relationships come with a lot of grey areas and there is never a clear-cut black and white. And even while you are with the person who is everything to you, perhaps deep down there is always something that is not revealed, and hence the shrouds. It is a painting which makes you stop in your tracks, think and reflect about the relationships we form with the ones we are closest to, the things that we do not even dare think, let alone voice.

Maybe this unattainable something is what causes poets and musicians to compose soulful renditions. Adele sings about how a kiss set fire to the rain. Seal sings about a kiss from a rose on the grey, which gives him pleasure and power and yet it is also his pain. But it is Elvis Presley who, I think, gets it right in the song *Kiss Me Quick,* in which he asks for a kiss while the feeling still remains, because the future comes with uncertainties and love can vanish, leaving one hurting, longing and with an emptiness that refuses to go away.

Finding and keeping love online and long-distance relationships

KAVYA, A YOUNG GIRL in her mid-twenties, came over the other evening and she was sad as the guy she was in love with had got a plum posting in Singapore and had moved. Even though they had talked about being in touch, she was missing him a lot.

'It's okay, Singapore is just four hours away. It's not like he is moving to the US. Now not only would that be a different time zone, it would also be about eighteen hours away, not to mention you would get only a few hours a day to connect because it would be night there and day here or vice versa,' I consoled her, trying to think of all the plus points in her situation.

'It's a kind of left-handed optimism,' she commented.

'I know, but it's not like we have a great right hand here,' I said.

'Long-distance relationships are really hard. Out of sight, out of mind,' she was glum and inconsolable.

'Look, it's all in your mind really,' I said, refusing to indulge her in the self-pity mode that she seemed to have descended into.

One of the greatest blessings of living in the times that we do is that the world has shrunk. In less than twenty-four hours, you can be in a different country, different continent and a different world altogether. At the click of a button you can seamlessly merge worlds and no matter what time zone you are in, you can always be connected.

In such a scenario, where countries are compressed like a zip file, it is no surprise that the way we find love and sustain it has evolved and changed. Earlier, we were networked via person to person. There was always an elderly aunt or mother's friend who would know someone who knew someone else who had an adult child who was single and ready to mingle. But today aunts and grandmas have been replaced by apps and websites.

Finding love through online dating sites is now one of the most popular ways that couples meet in today's technology-dominated world. The online dating industry was expected to generate 2.1 billion US dollars in revenue in 2014. A couple of years back it was only those people who felt they had no other recourse who went online to meet potential romantic partners. But with the invasion of technology the stigma associated with meeting people online has reduced significantly. Research shows that more than one-third of married couples in the UK and US have met online.

Today the choices young people have are unlimited. There are apps like Tinder where you swipe right for like, left for dislike and you end up meeting a person for a quick or slow (depending on how you like it) session of you-know-what. But, this is not for a long-term relationship and is at best superficial. If you are looking for that elusive Mr or Ms Right, there are many apps for that too. Twine Canvas is a dating app that lets you explore mutual interests and you get to know the person a little better as you compare personalities instead of pictures. You can choose to remain anonymous while chatting with the other person. You can choose when you want to reveal your picture, make a connection, take things further or make a graceful exit.

In fact Kavya had met her boyfriend online on a hiking forum. They initially emailed each other; then when they got to know each other better, they exchanged phone numbers and began chatting, still without having met. Many conversations later, they finally met and things had gone so well, they moved in together.

For every wonderful *aww*-inducing online love story though, there are several awful ones. One never knows who one is interacting with. In a connected world, hiding behind masks, fake profiles and names and creating compelling personas is as easy as rustling up a meal of instant noodles. A few minutes are all it takes and the game is on. You can be whoever you want to be. You do not have to dress up, make an effort or even step out of the house. A friend of mine confessed how she had wasted hours and hours online chatting with a guy who seemed suitable, but each time she wanted to meet, he kept making excuses that seemed genuine. He managed to avoid meeting her for a couple of months. When she began to insist that they should meet, he abruptly cut off all contact from her and vanished. Websites have tried to eliminate the probability of this happening. For instance, there is a site called 'Jess meet Ken', where a woman can 'recommend' or post the profile of a male friend who may not be right for her but could be great for someone else. The website says that there is a real Jess and a real Ken and they are now married with three children, and this, in fact, was how they met. Since the profiles here are recommended by people, the chances of creeps interacting with you is minimised.

Just like the dating apps that are customised to suit your needs, the choices for being connected today are unlimited. Just the other day I was messaging a friend in the UK. I had sent her a message on Viber, but the notifications told me that she hadn't seen it. So I logged into Skype, saw her online and then asked her to check Viber. Later, I emailed her, asking her if she had read my message as her Viber notifications seemed to have been turned off. She responded on WhatsApp and we ended up simultaneously instant messaging each other over Skype as well as Viber!

I met Kavya again after a few weeks and this time she seemed happier and more cheerful.

'You seem to have now adjusted to being away from him and you seem so much more at peace,' I remarked.

'Yes, I've realised that there are a few simple things that one can do to help when in a long-distance relationship, and that has made all the difference,' she said.

Naturally I insisted that she share with me how they managed. She said that they had spoken at length about it and set some ground rules in place. One of them was that they wish each other good morning and good night every single day. 'You will be surprised how much of a difference a tiny thing like that makes when you are miles away from each other,' she said.

Then they started sharing short video clips and snaps. When he had an office party, he sent her a short clip and she felt she was right there, living in the moment with him. When a plant that she was growing bloomed, she sent him snaps. Throughout the day, they sent each other short emails. Over the weekend, they chatted on Skype, sometimes indulging in some dirty talk. They were very honest with each other about the feelings of loneliness and jealousy that crept up from time to time. In short, they were always connected. She also said that now that they were apart, it made them value their time together more. She had already booked her tickets to Singapore for a long weekend coming up, and had got cheap fares. Her boyfriend's contract would come to an end in two years, and she felt they could manage till then.

'It isn't as bad as I thought. In fact, with these things that we are now doing, it is even better!' she confessed.

Oh, the times we live in. No matter what your quest, the internet has got your back. There's someone for everyone and in this connected world, you never need be alone. You just have to make an extra effort to stay connected. The options are only as limited as your imagination.

How Tinder changed Valentine

It was the month of February and there was no escaping the most important day of the month. Yes, Valentine's.

With Valentine's Day preparations gathering momentum all around us like a particularly large balloon being inflated for a children's birthday party, there was going to be no respite from the tacky hearts, splashes of red and declarations of undying love through every medium possible for the next two weeks. Each year, the real frenzy starts a week before V-day, with each successive day being declared as Rose Day, Propose Day, Chocolate Day, Teddy Day, Promise Day, Kiss Day, Hug Day and finally the queen mother of all—Valentine's Day.

Until recently I was only vaguely aware of the existence of Valentine's Day, with it stirring a few memories of the time I was in college and all of us used to dress in red and wait with bated breath to see which guy would send us a Valentine's Day card. I distinctly remember the year when about fourteen girls in my class were all delighted at having received a dozen red roses. They were all very excited until they compared notes and discovered that it was the same guy who had sent similar cards to all fourteen girls! I guess he was hedging his bets—out of the fourteen chosen ones, even if one said yes, he would be content. I don't know if he was foolish or smart but he was crazy for sure.

Today, I see my timeline on my social media pages flooded with various days prefixed with names of various things cute, and tons of pictures of satisfied twenty-somethings and teeny boppers posing with their cherished treasures of roses, teddies and what not, declaring gratitude and happiness to be loved so much. Welcome to modern-day Valentine's—where the worth of your love is judged by the size of the teddy bear that you have been able to gift your loved one. (What, no teddy bear? You don't love me!)

The commercial enterprises cash in on this completely. Everything from pressure cookers to treadmills to real estate to lingerie has taken on a Valentine's Day spin. Do you love your wife? Surprise her with a pressure cooker this Valentine. Do you love your family? Gift them the perfect home this Valentine. I am certain St. Valentine, the saint who married off lovers in secret, never envisaged the way this celebration would turn out to be one of the biggest consumer holidays. Today an estimated one billion Valentine cards are sent out each year, which is more than on any other holiday, except for Christmas. More than thirty-five million heart-shaped boxes of chocolate are sold and more than two hundred and twenty million red roses are produced just for the holiday. In the US alone, about twenty billion dollars are spent on Valentine's Day. That the day holds great importance for those in love is corroborated by the fact that about six million couples are likely to get engaged on 14 February.

While all this expression of love via teddy bears is okay for those hopelessly in love, what about the singles who still haven't found 'The One'? Fret not, for the marketers, those clever people, haven't forgotten them at all. A pub in Dublin hosted a Tinder party for singles this Valentine's. They offered users of this dating app a free glass of champagne if they showed up at the bar and flashed their Tinder profile. Since other users of Tinder would be assembled there too, one could easily find a potential partner right there and you could be hooking up with someone on Valentine's Day. They called it 'Love Me Tinder' night, a play on one of the most popular love songs on Valentine's Day, Elvis Presley's *Love Me Tender*. Most people who dedicate that song to their partner would have gone through the various stages of romance like flirting, dating, courtship and finally the declaration of love. This takes a few months at the very least. But for those at the bar, in search of love or its alias, there is no need to wait. Romance here is manufactured with a single swipe—'I like you, you're it, let's hook-up, it's Valentine's Day', and you have a partner within moments of meeting each other.

At the other extreme are anti-Valentine's Day parties, such as the one hosted by a pub in Los Angeles, which had voodoo dolls, some piñata aggression-release therapy and prizes for the worst 'got-dumped' stories. Thus you had company if you were recently dumped, and you didn't have to sit at home brooding.

Whether you are in love or standing on the periphery waiting to jump in, or have escaped with singes or sometimes third-degree burns, there is a Valentine's just for you. I wouldn't be surprised if the local vegetable seller started packing potatoes and onions in heart-shaped baskets especially for Valentine's Day. After all, it is a splendid marketing opportunity and no true-blue salesman would let go of the chance to jump on the bandwagon and peddle his ware, laced with hearts and the promise of everlasting love.

Never mind what happens later. The hope of finding that elusive thing is the fuel we all thrive on.

What to do when you are friend-zoned

IT WAS THE MONTH of August and the festival of Raksha Bandhan had just gone by. A friend of mine was visiting me and we were discussing how, when we were in school, it felt like the end of the world for a guy if a girl he had a crush on approached him with a rakhi in her hand. My friend commented that it was the Indian version of the 'Let's be friends' or 'I love you but I am not *in* love with you' scenario.

The worst nightmare for many young guys is to be 'friend-zoned' by a girl they hope to have a relationship with. He then becomes her go-to guy for all her boyfriend troubles, the male point-of-view and general advice-seeking, and he burns as he watches her confess her feelings for another guy. The same could happen with a woman too, where a guy declares her as his best buddy, and goes on to tell her about his crushes, while the girl patiently listens to him, hoping that he gets a hint about the giant-sized crush she has on him, all the time nodding understandingly as he oohs and aahs about the hotness quotient, mental compatibility and other things that he seeks in other women, not her.

What to do when you are friend-zoned

The dreaded friend-zone is a situation where there is dissimilarity in romantic feelings between two individuals. One of them wants more out of the friendship while the other is not in the same place. This zone creates feelings of inadequacy for one of the parties because the emotional or physical needs of one of them are not being met. One of them is content and the other is not. One of the parties is putting their all into this relationship, expecting something different from what they are now receiving.

Being stuck in the friend-zone can be hard as there is no apparent reason to break off what is probably a great friendship. And yet it is painful each time the person talks about someone else. The fact is, nobody owes anyone either their time or their body unless they themselves feel happy about sharing it. One cannot compel someone to feel attracted to you or love you, unless they themselves want to. In the friend-zone, the boundaries are drawn even before the person has had a chance to make a move, and to break through this barrier can be tricky if not downright impossible.

If you find yourself slotted into a friend zone, there are a few things that you can do to try and get out of this slot.

The very first thing you have to do is stop acting like their boyfriend/girlfriend when you aren't. Deep down you may be elated when they call you to go out for a movie or for a shopping trip, and there might be nothing more you want. However, if you are available to them *all* the time, like a sibling, then that is how you will be treated. Start going on dates with other people. If they are interested in you, they are sure to notice your absence and will want something more. Also, it gives you a chance to get to know other people—and who knows, they might turn out to be really interesting and there may be sparks flying.

Another thing that you can do is start flirting with them. Pay them compliments which are sincere but not over-the-top. Telling someone that you love the perfume that they are wearing is 'not crossing the line', and yet sensual. Start breaking the usual pattern of communication. If you have a certain comfort level with them, chances are you have slipped into 'friend-mode'. Try and break that mode by sending out hints that you want to take it further. If they are interested in you or have similar thoughts in their head, then they will definitely pick up the vibes when you change your behaviour.

A third thing that you can do is a bold step which you have to brace yourself to take. You could ask them out for a date. The worst that can happen here is them laughing and asking if you are kidding. (Yes, the very thought is mortifying, I know. But nothing ventured, nothing gained!) If they do, tell them you are not, and suggest a fun activity for the date, where you are certain they will have fun. For example, if you know she likes yoga, suggest a day out at an Ayurvedic spa with yoga thrown in. Or if you know that he enjoys trekking, plan an impromptu hike to a place which is interesting. When you do things together that you both enjoy, it is bound to ignite sparks.

In situations where you are friend-zoned, it is best to come clean early on in the relationship. The longer you take, the harder it will get. As difficult as it may be to confess that you want more out of the relationship, it is important that this is done as soon as feelings other than friendship develop. Most people do not do it from the fear of rejection, and also because they are scared to disturb an existing relationship where at least a part of their needs are met.

In the 2005 romantic comedy *Just Friends*, directed by Roger Kumble, the protagonist Chris, played by Ryan Reynolds, sets out to get out of this friend-zone which he has been boxed into by Jamie, played by Amy Smart. Chris has already been rejected by Jamie years ago in high school, and he is now a hot-shot record producer in Hollywood. He gets a chance to woo her all over again, and he does all he can to get out of the friend-zone. In the popular sitcom *Friends*, in the episode, 'The One with the Blackout', Joey (Matt LeBlanc) describes Ross (David Schwimmer), who is in love with Rachel (Jennifer Aniston) as 'The mayor of the friend zone'. The viewers found the storyline of Ross and Rachel dramatically compelling, watching week after week to see if he would ever escape the 'friend zone' or date other women.

In real life too there are many Rosses and Rachels, stuck in this zone, afraid to make the first move in case they are rejected and hanging onto the coat-tails of friendship even though it is a torture they endure day after day. The heart has its reasons and the mind has its ways. Sometimes, even after expressing your interest, even after going out for dates and even after showering them with compliments and flirting with them, they may still not want you as a romantic partner. In such cases, it is best to let go with grace. Not every relationship is meant to be.

A relationship is a fine dance, with both parties being privy to—and willing participants in—complex codes and secret mental games, which only the people involved can decipher. Sometimes one of them gets the cues wrong and the box of the friend-zone closes in faster than you can say When-Harry-met-Sally. Whether they break out of it or not is up to them.

As the popular tagline of the movie goes: Some friends are just friends. Others you get to see naked.

How to tell if it is love or lust

'How can I be sure that it is love, not lust? After all, she is an incredibly attractive woman and I am drawn to her physically,' Amit said.

'How can you not know if it is love? Have you never been in love before?' I asked him.

'I have, but I wondered then too,' was his reply.

'Love just *feels* different,' I answered.

'How? Can you explain?' he was persistent. And confused. He had never before been in a relationship in which he had feelings of this intensity. He had met her at his first job and they were colleagues, working together on the same project. He hadn't really spoken to her about it and he wanted to be sure of what he felt before making a decision to take it to the next level. After all, at twenty-six, both he and his colleague were what their parents considered to be a 'marriageable age'.

So I told him a true story which takes us back to the early Eighties, the pre-internet days, when I was about eleven years old. My parents used to pass on every New Year card they received to me and I would hoard them, admiring the pretty pictures, the glossy paper and sometimes the quotes that were printed on them. One year I came across a New Year card that had a picture of a lone cat perched on a cushion near a windowsill, looking outside. The caption on the card read: *Love does not consist in gazing at each other, but looking outward in the same direction.*

It made me think and I asked my father if a cat—or any animal for that matter—could fall in love, or was love an emotion unique only to humans. My father replied that animals have been known to show attachment and love. He told me the story of Greyfriars Bobby, whose statue sits in Edinburgh, near George IV Bridge.

Bobby was a skye terrier that belonged to a policeman, Constable John Gray, who worked for the Edinburgh city police. The two were inseparable and worked on police duty as a team. In October 1857, Gray caught a nasty cough which later developed into tuberculosis. He passed away in December the same year, even as Bobby lay at his feet. For fourteen years after that, Bobby sat faithfully by his master's grave, keeping vigil, waiting for him, until his own death in 1872.

Scientists agree that animals are capable of experiencing the same range of emotions that humans do. Just like humans, animals too form deep feelings of attachment. The brains of many mammals are surprisingly similar to the human brain.

But what differentiates humans from their animal counterparts is the complexity of the relationships that we form. For animals it is simple. If they love somebody they express it. If your dog is happy to see you, it is evident by the wag in his tail. If an animal wants to have sex with another, then they engage in a specific mating ritual which may or may not culminate in copulation. Animals do not wonder about long-term commitments, whether it will last, or if it is a one-night stand.

For us humans, it is a little more complicated. We wonder about our feelings. We think about whether it is love or lust that we are experiencing. We slot our relationships into an array of categories ranging from a simple 'boyfriend-girlfriend' and 'committed', to the slightly complicated and hard-to-understand 'f-buddies' and 'married but looking'. With a plethora of choice, how can we distinguish love from lust and how can we tell if that attractive person checking us out just wants a quick roll in the hay or something more? This was precisely Amit's dilemma.

The social scientists pondered this and found that it is difficult to disentangle romantic love and sexual desire. In order to tell what was which, they studied the brain and discovered that love and sexual desire each activated a different area of the brain. Thus, if you are sexually attracted to someone, it is a different part of your brain cells that are working as opposed to when you are romantically attracted. But they wanted a simpler way to tell the difference and hence they narrowed it down to something easily observable—eye movements.

In a study conducted by Chicago University's departments of psychiatry and psychology, in association with the University of Geneva, participants were shown different full-length photographs of people, none of which contained nudity, and were asked to classify whether they elicited feelings of sexual desire or feelings of love. Simultaneously, their eye-movements were tracked. What they discovered was that as soon as participants saw a photograph, their brains were immediately able to identify whether it was romantic love or sexual interest but it happened at a very subconscious level without the participants themselves being aware of it. But there was a significant shift in their eye movement when there was sexual desire involved. If they were experiencing only romantic love, then their gaze tend to be fixated on the face. However if there was sexual desire, it tended to wander towards the rest of the body. It was the same for male and female participants.

And now that I am an adult, I think the words on that card that I had seen in childhood can be modified to say: 'Love does not consist in looking at each other's body parts, but in holding each other's gaze.'

I mentioned all of this to Amit and he nodded. He said things made sense to him now and he knew what it was.

After all, the eyes speak their own secret language of love.

How music affects love

How many times has a song taken you right back to high school days, evoking memories of your crush playing it for you or dedicating it to you? If you are anything like me, I bet it has happened many times. Sometimes a song I hear on the radio takes me back to the days when we used to have tape recorders and cassettes. Anyone who has grown up in the Eighties will distinctly remember the spool of tape and the all-useful pencil which was an indispensable tool to wind cassettes. We would also frantically press the 'pause button' to write down lyrics of a song as they weren't readily available in the pre-internet era. Often we misheard the lyrics and we made up our own versions of what we thought the lyrics could be. Thus the line in the popular song by The Cure, *Friday I'm in Love* became 'fried egg I'm in love' and the line in U2's song *With or Without You*, which goes 'sleight of hand and twist of fate' became 'slice of ham and piece of cake'; and we sang along loudly, strumming our air guitars, pretending to be rock stars. I secretly wondered why someone would tell a fried egg they were in love and why anyone would talk about ham and cake in a love song. I never expressed this, but pretended I understood the lyrics perfectly and nodded to the music in order to appear 'cool'.

No matter where we live, what ethnicity we are, or what our profession, we all have music that we totally love and some that we cannot bear to hear for even five minutes. While some of us are active listeners who cannot imagine life without an iPod, others will groove to anything the local radio station plays on their morning commute to work. And then there are others for whom music is a necessity to get through chores like cooking, doing the laundry and walking on the treadmill.

Researchers have found that listening to music that we love causes a dopamine surge in our bodies—the same feel-good chemical that is released when we fall in love, have sex or eat food rich in salt. Powerful music is that which evokes the deepest of emotions in us, which explains why so many people cry listening to an opera even when they don't understand the language it is in.

In the film *The Shawshank Redemption*, a personal favourite of mine and one that appears in several 'top 100 films of all time' lists, there is a scene where Andy Dufrense, played by Tim Robbins, broadcasts a piece of Italian opera on the prison's public address system. Every single prisoner stops what he is doing and listens to it, and in that bit of music they experience a brief glimpse of freedom, hope and happiness—something they all crave for. The prison warden knocks on the door, asking Andy to stop the music, but instead he turns up the volume, sits back and revels in it, even though he knows the punishment that he is bound to get will be harsh. The narrator says, 'I have no idea to this day what those two Italian ladies were singing about. Truth is, I don't want to know. Some things are best left unsaid. I like to think that it was something so beautiful it can't be expressed in words and makes your heart ache because of it.'

Music grabs our emotions instantly in a way that no other form of art can. To appreciate art, especially if it belongs to the surrealist or modernist genre, we need to study it, think about it and only then can we respond to it. But a catchy beat, even if it is Yo-Yo Honey Singh crooning, can set your foot tapping inadvertently.

Music also helps people connect very quickly. In a study conducted in the US, participants were paired off (same sex and opposite sex) and told to get to know each other over a period of six weeks. It was found that in the very first week, 58 per cent of the discussions were about music they liked, compared to 37 per cent of other categories that included books, TV shows and films. We are able to easily connect and bond with those who like the same music as us, because the type of music we like expresses something about ourselves.

Music and love are inextricably linked. Adele's hit *Someone Like You* was composed after the guy she was in love with walked out of her life. It is hard to listen to her talking about it, and then singing it at Royal Albert Hall, without being moved to tears. (I urge you to watch the version with speech and public reaction on YouTube, if you haven't already.) The album went on to sell more than twenty-eight million copies worldwide. In Bollywood films, the hero bursts into song to express his love for the heroine as they run through mustard fields and dance on top of trains to the accompaniment of musicians who have magically appeared to make the experience more colourful, which only a true-blue Indian would understand and forgive.

An experiment was conducted in a university in France, where single women in the age group of eighteen to twenty were exposed to either romantic or neutral music while waiting to meet a young male they'd been told was visiting them for a marketing survey. During a break in the survey, the young man asked the participant for her phone number. It was found that women previously exposed to the romantic music complied with the request more readily than those exposed to the neutral music. The percentage of women who agreed to a date almost doubled from 28 to 52 per cent after they had listened to romantic music.

All lovers know how much significance the words, 'Listen carefully to the lyrics of this song', convey. After all, it is music which expresses things that words cannot convey and it takes them to a place where nothing matters but the two of them.

On making a relationship last through the years

WHO CAN ESCAPE THE clutches of love? Right from adolescents to young folks who have just found financial freedom and begun to live away from their parents, from the middle-aged to the old and even married folks—nobody is immune to it. It can strike at any time and slowly draw you in and before you realise it, there is that certain somebody in your life the mere mention of whose name lights up your world. You have never felt anything like it before and you are swept away in the delirium, blissful, happy, contented.

If you are an adult, chances are that you have been in love at least once in your life and you know how it makes you feel like Superman minus the costume. When in love, the dopamine—a neurotransmitter in your brain—goes on overdrive, releasing a lot of feel-good hormones like oxytocin, phenylethylamine and a few other unpronounceable names. The chemicals combine to give you a natural high, making you see only what is great in the relationship. Everything instantly seems brighter, larger than life and in clear, sharp, high-definition focus, like suddenly discovering clarity with new glasses after viewing the world through myopic, hazy eyes for many years. The newly-chosen one is perfect in every respect and even their quirks are adorable.

Talks on the telephone stretch into hours, the conversation flowing smoother than the finest silk with a phone bill to match. You feel like there is nothing that can go wrong in this relationship, and you tell your friends who aren't already bored of listening to you droning on about how perfect this is and how very fortunate you are.

Experts say that this stage can last anything from two months to two years. If things have gone smoothly during this time period, you might find yourself living together or, in most cases, married. (After all, what is there to wait? This is undoubtedly 'The One' you want to spend the rest of your life with.)

Then creeps up the stage where the blinkers dissolve. Gradually, the neurotransmitters slow down and the brain stops producing the happy-hormones. This is where reality sets in and the fights start. Living together leads to the discovery of many hitherto unknown aspects of the 'perfect person', and the newly-discovered traits are not always in sync with your way of doing things. The earlier 'Sweetie, wet towel on the floor, don't worry, I will get it' changes to 'Grrr … I always clear up after you'.

If the relationship has survived the assault of harsh reality and the not-so-harmonious adjustments that come along with living together and the blinkers-off stage, then the couple is on their way to sturdier grounds. However, one cannot be complacent that it is now a happily-ever-after, as this stage comes with its dangers too.

Sometimes the dangers are in the form of attractive colleagues with whom out-station trips on work are unavoidable, and sometimes they are in the form of an old flame you presumed was relegated to history, but with whom contact has now been rekindled by a casually dropped, 'Hey, didn't we go to college together', message thanks to social media, which lets one track down almost anybody, except perhaps Rip Van Winkle (and perhaps him too, if you care to look hard enough).

That was what happened with Shyla and Vishwanath. Both had studied together in the same school twenty years back, which was when they had last met. Shyla's memories of Vishwanath were of him as a tall, lanky seventeen-year-old, taking charge of things easily, and teaming up with her as they were both house captains. Vishwanath recalled Shyla in pigtails and as a very efficient co-house captain. After they finished their 12th standard, Vishwanath had gone abroad for his studies and Shyla had moved to Delhi, where her father had got a posting. Those were the pre-internet times and they lost touch; they had vowed to write letters to each other, but these had become a trickle after the initial few months. Gradually they both moved on with their lives.

They reconnected over Facebook when their school began plans for a twentieth-year reunion. Shyla was now married and mother to a seven-year-old. Vishwanath had two children, a five-year-old and a three-year-old. They had a lot of catching up to do, and were delighted to speak on the phone. Shyla came home excitedly and told her husband about it; and Vishwanath too was eager to share with his wife the news of reconnecting with Shyla. They met at the school reunion and the connection between them was very evident to everyone around them.

After they parted ways, they found that they couldn't stay away from each other and chatted constantly on instant messengers. Shyla discovered a new side to herself. She loved talking to Vish and found that she was sharing with him much more than what she shared with her husband. Vish, on his part, was drawn in without even realising it. They continued this for a while till Shyla realised how distant it was making her from her husband. She found herself mentally comparing her husband to Vish and picking fights with her husband for the silliest of things. She thought about it for a few days and decided that the only way for her to save her marriage was to put an end to her messaging Vish, which is what she did. She knew that had she not done it, things would have deteriorated further and they would have definitely headed for a divorce. Shyla was certain she didn't want that, and was mature enough to realise the harm that it was causing her marriage, and hence she was able to apply the brakes to the relationship with Vish, in time, before it was too late.

Whether you decide to go amber, green or red with these distractions or remain true-blue to your now-not-so-perfect chosen one, with whom you have to spend the rest of your life, will be a decision you agonise over. If you ignore your call from the past, you might be left with an unfinished longing of what-if, and if you proceed there is a very real danger of it exploding into something far beyond your control, and you risk losing what you have nurtured and built over several years. Sometimes you discover that the clear blue stream of youth existed only in your imagination. The waters are muddier and murkier than ever before and it was safer to stay on known shores than to risk exploring. If your little amorous adventures are discovered by the spouse, the relationship faces another storm and is put to further tumultuous tests.

Statistical studies reveal that, globally, the chances of a divorce are highest between the fourth and eight wedding anniversaries. These stages are not linear or gradient; rather, they are fluid. Each stage blends into another; with couples learning lessons from it, possibly returning to previous ones, and then moving on. Also, the possibility of a divorce is very much prevalent in all stages, much like the sword of Damocles.

If all the above are navigated safely, as Shyla did in her marriage, congratulations are in order, as you have made it to the 'we are a team' stage. At this point, you have accepted your partner with all their flaws and weaknesses, and you understand you are never going to succeed in changing them. Yet you choose to be with them, and for the first time the clichéd saying 'Love changes everything' begins to make new sense.

Is our love for someone immortal?

'GOD, HE ACTS LIKE he is the first person who has been in love. It's like he is the Christopher Columbus of love or something,' groaned Rahul. He was talking about his flatmate, who had been constantly telling him about how marvellous, witty and charming his girlfriend was, and how they could talk for hours. Rahul was happy for him and hoped they would get hitched soon. 'At least that would mean an end to the torture that I have to undergo any time that he is not on the phone with her,' he quipped.

Some months later, I remembered his Christopher Columbus friend and asked him how the couple were doing.

'Oh, it's all under control now,' he said.

'How? What happened? Did they split up?' I asked.

'No, they did not. The usual happened,' he said. 'They got married. And now they hardly talk.'

I couldn't help chuckling.

Like all stories, love stories too come to an end. There are some that end in marriage, which could mean a new modified version of love-as-we-knew-it, and then there are others that wither, wane and wilt under the assault of life's realities, like a new job, a relocation, or sometimes even a new entrant into the lives of the respective parties. Then there is a third kind. These are the ones that get immortalised in poems, works of art, literature and history, and they are talked about even after centuries.

Love stories do not recognise age, caste or the marital status of those that are hit by Cupid's arrow. Napoleon's love for Josephine is well-known and documented too. Many of the letters he wrote her still exist. (Although I am certain that at the time of writing those letters they would have never even dreamt that an exchange so intimate would at some point of time be displayed publicly.) Josephine was a much older woman, a widow with two children. Napoleon's family did not approve of her but that didn't stop the lovers. In one of his letters Napoleon writes about how his happiness lies in being near her. He pines for her and says that ever since he left her he has been constantly depressed. He writes, *'When, free from all solicitude, all harassing care, shall I be able to pass all my time with you, having only to love you, and to think only of the happiness of so saying, and of proving it to you?'*

One of my favourite love stories is narrated by Alfred Noyes in his beautiful poem 'The Highwayman', which tells the story of Beth who fell in love with a brigand. He meets Beth for a single kiss, promising her that he will be back the following night and that nothing can stop him. He asks Beth to wait for him by the moonlight. The next night, however, it is a group of soldiers that turn up at her door. They tie her up, with a gun at her chest and drink beer as they await the highwayman; they plan to shoot him when he arrives. Beth quietly struggles till she has her finger on the trigger of the gun, which the soldiers are not aware of. She stays alert till she hears the clattering of the hooves of the horse of her lover. She fires the gun, thus warning him of the ambush, giving up her life for him. The highwayman charges towards the soldiers with his rapier brandished, but they manage to kill him. Noyes describes how the highwayman's ghost still rides down the highway on a full-moon night to meet Beth.

Yet another tragic love story is that of Sir Lancelot and Queen Guinevere. Sir Lancelot was loyal, wise and kind, and one of the best knights that King Arthur had. However he fell in love with the king's wife, Queen Guinevere. At first Guinevere tried to ignore her feelings, as did Lancelot his, for they knew how inappropriate it was. But they couldn't fight it for long—the heart has its own reasons and carves its own path. Over a period of time they became lovers, meeting in secret, enjoying stolen moments. Before long, rumours started flying and one night, King Arthur's nephew gathered twelve knights and stormed into Guinevere's chambers, catching her in bed with Sir Lancelot. An enraged King Arthur attacked Lancelot's castle but failed to capture him. The lovers never saw each other again. Sir Lancelot ended up spending his last days as a hermit and Guinevere became a nun at Amesbury, where she died. Lord Alfred Tennyson immortalised their story in his poem 'Sir Lancelot and Queen Guinevere', in which he talks of souls that balance love and pain.

There are also many works of art that depict this story, the most well-known of which is by Herbert James Draper, which shows a very beautiful Guinevere surrounded by her maids and helpers. Sir Lancelot is in the foreground, gazing at her with love in his eyes.

Which love stories of our times will be talked about hundreds of years from now remains to be seen. But one thing is clear: when it comes to love, nothing has changed. Like the line in the movie *Interstellar* goes: love is the one thing that we're capable of perceiving that transcends dimensions of time and space.

GETTING HITCHED

Stand together, yet not too near together: for the pillars of the temple stand apart. And the oak tree and the cypress grow not in each other's shadow.
–Kahlil Gibran

I don't want to be married just to be married. I can't think of anything lonelier than spending the rest of my life with someone I can't talk to, or worse, someone I can't be silent with.
–Mary Ann Shaffer, The Guernsey Literary and
Potato Peel Pie Society

Why proposals are always on bended knees

NIKHIL HAS BEEN HUNTING for that perfect ring for the last few weekends. He has visited at least five jewellery shops, and he hasn't liked anything he's seen. He wants to pop the question to his girlfriend with whom he has been in a relationship for the last three years and he wants everything about the moment to be 'perfect', and hence the massive hunt.

I told him that had he been living a few centuries earlier, his task would not have been so difficult.

'How is that?' he asked.

'Based on where you were living, you could gift her many objects, not necessarily a ring,' I answered.

He looked at me to see if I was joking. I wasn't.

If you were a woman living in medieval Europe in the 1800s, and a guy was interested in you, he would gift you a pair of gloves. If you wore it to church the next Sunday, it would signify that you had accepted his proposal. In Wales, a man who was interested in a woman would gift her a wooden spoon which he'd carved himself. If the lady accepted his proposal, she would wear it around her neck with a ribbon. In colonial

America the man sent the lady a thimble. If she wore it on her finger, then it was understood that she was his. Nikhil laughed when I told him this, picturing, he said, his girlfriend wearing a thimble instead of a diamond ring.

It was the Romans and the Egyptians who—around three thousand years ago— began the use of rings as a symbol of 'ownership' of the woman by her husband. The ring is a never-ending circle, thus indicating that the relationship is for eternity. And after all, when one is beginning a new relationship, that is what you hope for—for it to last forever. You do not expect reality to rear its ugly head once the courtship phase is over and the very real issues like managing children and a home arise.

If you were a woman in India around that period, you would be spared wearing a wooden spoon, a thimble or gloves. You would simply have no need for any of it as you would have been married off by your parents before you turned fourteen. It was only in 1872 that the minimum marriageable age for women was raised and fixed at fourteen for women and eighteen for men. It was as late as 1929 that the child marriage restraint act was passed, further raising the minimum age for marriage as eighteen for women and twenty-one for men. My own grandmother was married off at the age of eleven. My grandfather was about ten years older, which was the norm those days. My grandmother did not have a say in who she was marrying and I highly doubt if marriage was anything more than a new game for her. For her, marriage simply meant that she now had to move into a different house and live with a new set of people. She had to obey her elders and do as she was told. The question of any man courting her or expressing his love for her never arose. If you had told my grandmother that a guy will go down on bended knees to propose to a lady he loves, she would probably throw back her head and laugh. She would find the concept preposterous. 'Why in the world should a man do that?' she would ask in bewilderment.

It is not known how or where the tradition of going down on a bended knee while asking for a woman's hand in marriage began. In several religious ceremonies, kneeling during prayer was common. So was kneeling while accepting an award from a king or a queen. A gentleman would also go down on one knee while accepting a proposal and making a commitment. Gradually this extended to romantic encounters too, and men began going down on one knee to declare their intention of making a woman their wife. It came to be associated with respect, commitment and honour. It would usually be done with the consent of the girl's parents.

Movies of our times have a few iconic, unforgettable wedding proposal scenes. In *Love Actually,* Jamie (Colin Firth), a Brit, falls in love with his Portuguese housekeeper. He learns Portuguese and proposes to her in her native language. Unknown to him, she has been learning English, and she responds to him in that language. In *Gone with the Wind,* Rhett (Clark Gable) rushes to Scarlett (Vivien Leigh) as soon as her husband is killed and he goes down on a bended knee, saying, 'I can't go on all my life waiting to catch you between husbands.'

In a study conducted online, it was found that more than 80 per cent of men felt it was important to get a clear go-ahead from the girl's parents before popping the question. About 60 per cent of the women felt the same. More than 75 per cent of the men also felt it was necessary to go down on a bended knee and 47 per cent of the women said that the 'surprise' factor was very important.

Today we live in a wired world, where we have more 'friends' on our social networks than the total number of people we have ever met in our lives. We live in times where we decide whether we like someone enough to sleep with them or not by just a swipe on our touch-screen phones. And yet, it appears, when it comes to the all-important marriage proposal, which alters the relationship between two people forever, nothing seems to have changed.

And as for Nikhil—well, he found, the perfect ring and was elated with his purchase. He went down on bended knee and proposed to his girlfriend. She was thrilled and accepted. Only thing—the ring didn't fit her! But as long as they are both happy, that's what counts.

Finding the right person to marry

NISHIKA, A YOUNG SMART girl in her early twenties who has just started her career, is in a dilemma as her parents want her to get married and she wants to focus on her career and does not feel ready for marriage yet.

Saurabh, who is in his late twenties hasn't got married as he hasn't found the right person yet.

Mansi, a smart, brave young lady who has a great career going for her, called off her wedding after being engaged for five months as she realised that the guy was not right for her. I applauded her courage and her decision. Her folks and she suffered a huge loss monetarily as all the wedding arrangements had been made, the venue had been booked and wedding rings and other jewellery had been bought. Can you imagine the amount of courage this would have taken, especially in an Indian scenario? Her parents supported her decision completely and I was happy that she had the courage to call off her wedding rather than suffer with the wrong person simply to placate society. Not everyone can be as brave and as certain as she.

I have been doing some serious thinking about marriage. I know some bright young women in their late twenties and early thirties who are single and financially independent and leading their own lives. Yet 'well-meaning' relatives and parents push them like crazy to get married. Nothing you do as a woman counts unless you have got married and produced a child or two! I also know some really smart young men who are being pressured the same way. Somehow, in Indian society, everybody is content only if you are 'settled' (meaning married and have produced a child within two years of marriage) once you cross the age of twenty-five/twenty-six, whether you are a guy or a girl.

Often, with young men and women in India, what happens after they get a job and start earning is that many of their friends get married—perhaps succumbing to pressure from their families. They post 'happy couple' pictures on social networking sites, and congratulatory messages and 'oh, you are made for each other' kind of comments pour in. They find their own homes and move out of their bachelor(ette) pads. At the end of the day, they have 'someone to go home to'. All this sounds fantastically exciting when you're single.

But what most people do when they are looking for a person to marry is that they compromise simply because they feel time is running out, and 'everybody is getting married', and because parents and those well-meaning relatives will stop nagging. If the prospective match meets about 60 per cent of what one has in mind (after meeting several people who matched only 35-40 per cent, one gets fed up of searching for the perfect one too), they go ahead and say yes. Everyone

Finding the right person to marry

is ecstatic for a few days and congratulations start streaming in.

Trouble usually starts after around five-six months of knowing each other really well. Doubts then creep up and it makes one wonder if this is the right person to marry. The thing is, one can never be a hundred per cent certain. There is bound to be a little apprehension and a little fear. After all, you are treading into unknown territory.

Marriage is usually a lifetime of adjustments and compromises. Sometimes they work out and at other times, while they are not serious enough to warrant a divorce, they are irritating enough to ruin your peace of mind. Marriage then becomes a cross to carry—a doomed if I do and doomed if don't kind of a situation.

'So is there really something called the "right person"?' asked Nishika. 'And how do you know whether he is the right person for you? Or how does he know if I am the right girl for him?' She fired off the questions in quick succession eagerly scouring my face for answers. After all, I was older and, according to her, wiser—but mostly I think she was in awe that I have now been married for twenty years (yes, to the same person).

I didn't want to let her down and I decided to tell her honestly what I felt.

The frank answer to that question is: 'Marriage is a risk that you take, hoping you will grow together as individuals.' Twenty years down the line, they might find that the pace of growth of both people and the trajectory their paths have taken aren't congruent at all. The couple may find that they are strangers living under the same roof. But that comes later. I think for every marriage to have a chance of success there has to be a certain amount of compatibility and similar interests to begin with.

Being in love is great, but research shows that it is not possible to sustain the same level of passion for extended periods of time without burning out. We have to remember that love is a trap that nature sets to get us to reproduce. When you first fall in love, it's oxytocin at work. Oxytocin is the 'cuddle hormone' that plays a great role in maternal bonding and sex. When you are under its spell, Mr Average-okay-guy becomes Mr Amazingly-perfect-cute-funny-charming guy. It takes at least two years of living together or a baby—whichever is earlier—for its effect to diminish.

Be clinical and analyse if you share the same values and have the same attitude to life. How important is money to you and to him? What about a sense of humour? Do you both find the same things funny? What about common interests? Do you both like books, sports, movies, watching television? How important is physical fitness to you? To him? After about four or five years of marriage, these are the things that will sustain you. What is his attitude towards pets? Is one of you an animal lover, and the other thinks that the best place for animals is in a zoo? If so, at some point of time, you are going to have a problem, unless you decide in advance that there will be no place for pets in your home, for life.

Don't go by what he looks like right now. Picture him ten years hence. He may have gone bald. The stress that he will face in his professional life will surely begin to take its toll. He may look older than he is. He may begin to grey. Those muscular arms that you fawn over right now may be replaced by sagging muscles. It is a scientifically-proven fact that, after the age of twenty, we begin to lose approximately a pound of muscle mass a year. Even people who regularly exercise lose approximately half a pound of muscle mass a year. Will you still love him no matter what he looks like? The same goes for her looks too. She may gain weight. She may lose her hair or chop it all off. She may lose her sex appeal. Her body will have stretch marks and cellulite. Will she still be beautiful in your eyes?

Watch how he behaves. Observe how he treats waiters at a restaurant. Make a note of how he behaves towards your male friends. Look at how he behaves with others—colleagues, shopkeepers, your women friends, his parents, his siblings. The same goes for guys. Watch what her attitude towards people is. Does she have a kind heart? Is kindness an important quality for you? Is she social, introverted, extroverted? Do you like her basic personality and nature?

Also examine your attitude towards children. Having children is no joke. It is extremely demanding of both partners. There will be major lifestyle changes that need to be made. There will be night after night of a bawling baby, cleaning poop, breastfeeding, changing diapers, bathing, vaccinations, and visits to doctors. By the end of it all, I think a visit to the supermarket would count as an evening out. I am sure many parents can relate. There is joy too in it—the awesome, overwhelming feeling when you first hold your newborn and the realisation that YOU are now totally and wholly responsible for another life, those little button eyes that adore you, those little humans who love you unconditionally and think you are better and prettier than Miss Universe, that absolutely fabulous hug makes it all worth it—provided he and you want the same thing.

One thing that women, especially in India, have to consider is whether he is the kind of man who will help you with the housework, or whether he is a typical pampered mama's boy who will not even step into the kitchen to make himself a cup of tea. It might seem very cute at the beginning of the relationship that he cannot cook, but, after having a baby, when you are exhausted, tired and want to be looked after, it will not seem so fun any more. Ten years hence, when he comes back tired from work, and your child (presuming that you both want children) declares that for a project the next day, they have been asked to bring crepe paper and aluminium foil, will he still go out with a smile and get it? Does he seem the kind who will patiently go through lessons with a child for an exam the next day? Will he uncomplainingly iron their school uniforms and fill their water bottles at six-thirty in the morning? Will he spend time with the children and be an equal partner in their physical and emotional development, alongside you? If so, you might want to grab that guy and turn a blind eye to all his other faults! That species is very hard to come by.

In the end, there are only so many points that one can consider and tick off. The fact is, marriage is a long journey with an ever-changing set of rules and a large amount of unpredictability. Nothing prepares you for the game of life. Things happen to us which change us in ways we never thought possible. Keeping a marriage going through all that is a lot of hard work.

If your partner has been there for you through the good times and the bad, and if you have been there for your partner and, years later, if you are still each other's best friend, then you have hit the jackpot. But how much are you willing to invest in a marriage, and do the positives outweigh the negatives that a marriage brings? Those remain the questions for which the only person with the correct answer is you.

How to tell if someone is too old or too young for you

AJIT IS IN LOVE with Sreeja, who is sixteen years older than him. He is convinced it is not a crush: he is twenty-eight and has been in several relationships, so he knows the difference between a crush and love. He says that when they are together, age really does not matter as wave-lengths and other parameters match. It is only society that thinks of the disparity in ages and magnifies it. He hates it when people refer to this as a 'cougar' relationship.

The term 'cougar' is commonly used to denote an older woman who dates younger men or is in a relationship with a younger man. The usage was popularised after a book by Valerie Gibson titled *Cougar: A Guide for Older Women Dating Younger Men* came out in 2001. Lexicographers credit its origin to a dating site started by two Canadian women in 1999, where older women could meet younger men. The story goes that the women who founded the website were told by their nephew that they were like cougars who hunted small defenceless animals, which led them to name their site 'cougardate'. The term became popular and mainstream over a period of time, and it also came to mean an attractive older woman.

Culturally, no matter which part of the world you are from, a relationship between an older woman and a younger guy always raises eyebrows. When Demi Moore and Ashton Kutcher—sixteen years her junior—went public with their relationship, the gossip mills worked overtime and talk shows went berserk with discussions, mostly centring on Kutcher being a 'toy-boy' and Moore the wicked witch who got lucky. Cougar is a term strongly smacking of sexism. It is interesting to note that if a woman does it, she is a hunter, preying on helpless, young guys, but when a man does it, it is associated with him 'being protective' or buying the girl goodies. Not only does it imply that an older woman is unattractive and the younger guy has no choice as he is the 'prey' and not an adult who is in a consenting relationship because he genuinely enjoys the company of the woman, but it also portrays women in a desperate light.

Ajit's situation made me think whether age played a huge role in relationships. Is it possible to have a perfectly compatible and loving relationship even if there is an extreme difference in ages?

In relationships, the age difference between two individuals has always been a matter which is considered when it crosses the boundaries of a casual friendship and slips into the relationship zone. When the internet first came to India and chat-rooms were the norm, one of the first questions asked was, 'ASL?' That is: age, sex, location?

'Age is just a number.'

'A man is as old as he looks. A woman is as old as she feels.'

'You can't help getting older, but you don't have to get old.'

All these thoughts on age, the last one by George Burns, sum up what different people have felt about that all important number—your age.

If you were a woman who was born two hundred years ago, the most natural thing for you to do would be to get married to a man older than you, stay at home, cook and raise children. In traditional matchmaking, the man tended to be a few years older than the woman as he had to be well-established in his chosen way of making a living, and had to be capable of providing for his wife. Women didn't have to worry about that. The expectation was that they would be taken care of by their husbands. Thus the man being older in relationships stems from a deep-rooted instinct to choose a more successful and stronger man over a young guy just learning the ropes.

But as more and more women started working, drawing in pay cheques as much as or sometimes more than the guys they came into contact with did, the lines gradually blurred. Age is now no longer a constraint in finding the right partner.

A popular men's magazine compiled a list of the ninety-nine most desirable women and one truth that emerged out of this list was that men found older women incredibly attractive. The reasons cited for this were many. Older women were more confident sexually, had more money, were likely to be better

How to tell if someone is too old or too young for you

conversationalists, and tended to be more practical. There was also less drama and they didn't play games as they were sure of what they wanted and hence made better dates. They were also likely to have been in more relationships than a younger woman, and men felt that they would appreciate a good guy when they came across one and wouldn't take them for granted.

When the question of who is too old for you and who is too young for you to date is asked, invariably the half-your-age plus seven rule comes up as an answer, whether you are a man or a woman. So if you are a forty-two-year-old woman, according to the 'rule', you can date any guy who is twenty-eight or older. If you are a man who is thirty, you can date a woman who is twenty-two or older.

Who made this rule up? Its origin is hard to pin down, but it finds mention in the 1953 film *The Moon is Blue,* where Maggie McNamara, twenty-two, asks her suitor who is thirty, 'Haven't you heard that the girl is supposed to be half the man's age plus seven?' This rule also finds mention in the popular television series *How I Met Your Mother*.

The exact opposite of this rule defines the upper age limit to determine the 'oldest person you can date'. Here you double your age and then subtract seven. Thus, according to the 'rule', if you are a thirty-two-year-old woman you shouldn't date a man who is older than fifty-seven.

I find that these 'rules' really cannot be applied to any and every relationship. For rules to be applicable, they have to be consistent. But these rules are not consistent as the pair grows older. To elucidate, let us take the case of a person who is currently forty-two. As per the rule, he cannot date someone who is twenty-eight. But when the person turns twenty-nine, then the pair qualifies to date as the other person is now forty-three. Thus, if this rule is followed strictly, a person can 'qualify' to date another who is older within just a year or two if their ages currently fall within an 'unaccepted' range. How can your personality or other parameters necessary for a good relationship actually change that much within such a short span?

Also, since the 'rule' emerged from popular culture, it can be safely discarded even if people quote it from time to time. Interestingly, social scientists and researchers say that this rule does not really reflect people's choices. In 2001, Dutch social psychologists led by Bram Buunk from the University of Groningen conducted a study where they approached people in public places—railway stations, malls, libraries—and asked them what age range they would consider appropriate for five types of relationships: casual sex, sexual fantasy, a serious one, falling in love and marriage. For the purpose of the study, they classified the ages of the anonymous respondents—an equal number of men and women—as in their twenties, thirties, forties, fifties and sixties. They found that women's preferences remained consistent over time. Most women preferred to date men their own age with a range of a few years younger to a few years older. For most men, though, the difference between their own age and the age they considered appropriate to date increased dramatically as they got older. Men in their forties and above all said that a woman in her twenties was okay for casual sex or sexual fantasies. Lower their involvement with the woman, lower the age. In other words, older men were okay having sex with a woman half their age, but women showed no such preference for younger guys.

Research proves that there is no biological reason that a woman has to be younger than a guy for a relationship to flourish. The maturity levels of people, irrespective of gender, cannot be determined by chronological age. It depends on how open-minded they are and what their exposure is. I know many seventy-year-olds who have wonderfully curious minds, are extremely fit and still have a zest for life. I know some people in their late thirties who are unfit, have lost their spark for life and aren't curious or interested in too many things. They don their weariness like a comfortable coat, rarely bothering to take it off, settling down to a life of domestic bliss and carrying on with life.

For a relationship to work, it has to be a match of wavelength, interests and outlook. You have to be able to converse with that person and share similar interests. Your core values and outlook to life are more important than how old each one is. There are many successful relationships with huge age disparities.

Ajit has come to realise this as his love for Sreeja has only grown over the years. In India, there are several celebrities who have married women older than them. Sachin and Anjali Tendulkar, Abhishek Bachchan and Aishwarya Rai Bachchan, Farhan and Adhuna Akhtar are all couples where the woman is older than her partner. Other than celebrities, I know a few couples where there is at least a twelve-year age gap between the spouses (the woman being older) and their marriages are successful. What would probably matter in such relationships is how effectively the couple deals with society and also their parents, as the relationship is unconventional for sure. As long as the couple in question is comfortable with each other and confident about it, there is no reason why it shouldn't work out.

Ultimately, what enables a great relationship to flourish is not how old each one is but how much they love each other. After all, love knows no age.

And when it comes to age, among all the quotes, Mark Twain seems to have got it right when he said, 'Age is a question of mind over matter. If you do not mind, it does not matter.'

Does marriage take away your freedom?

SEEMA IS THIRTY-TWO AND in a committed relationship. She and her boyfriend don't plan on getting married though; neither sees the need. They have decided that they do not want any children and they both hate the thought of doing something just to please society. They are completely secure about their relationship. They have been living together for a couple of years now and both are content and happy in their respective careers. They travel a lot, do a lot of things together and are happy with each other. Theirs is an unusual arrangement for sure, at least in India, where the pressure from parents and society starts as soon as you find a good job and begin to live on your own. The all-important relatives try and matchmake, as do friends, and a decision like Seema's and that of her partner is impossible to explain to people with a predominantly Indian middle class mindset where the goal is college, job, marriage and children.

Many people I know in their late twenties do not want to get married at all. The world over, marriage statistics are on the decline. In the US, one in five people have never been married at the age of twenty-five and this is up from one in ten in 1960. In India, the average age of first marriage is twenty-six for men and twenty-two for women (data from year 2011 census). India is one of the countries with the lowest age of first marriage. In the UK, the average age is thirty-two for men and thirty for women (2010), and the country with the highest average age of first marriage is Sweden, where it goes up to thirty-five for men and thirty-three for women (2011).

When it comes to marriage, a common joke that does the rounds goes, 'I am the boss of the house and I have my wife's permission to say so.' A cartoon that shows a hassled middle-aged man says, 'In our home, I make all the important decisions like deciding which political party is better, how to save the environment and things like that. The minor things like which movie to watch, where to eat out, where to take a family holiday and how much to spend are all decided by my wife.' These cartoons are funny because what is expressed in them strikes a chord with most people who are married. A long time back, much before I was married, a colleague at my workplace told me that 95 per cent of men are afraid of their wives. As a young unmarried girl, I had found that statement a bit nonsensical and had argued with him. 'How can you be afraid of someone you love? I am presuming there is some love if both of you want to spend the rest of your lives together,' I had said. 'Marriage is not so easy and, many a time, it is best to hold your silence if you don't want fights,' he replied. I found it a bit hard to understand then.

But today, I would amend his statement to say that 95 per cent of men know what to say and what not to say when their wives are around. It would be the same for wives too. Living together for a long time teaches you to tweak your thoughts, expectations and opinions as you learn how to keep harmony as you navigate that ship called marriage.

One of the main arguments people have against marriage is that it takes away your freedom. When one is single, every decision is your own. You do not have to ask anyone before you give a gift to a friend, make a dinner date or decide to go out for a movie with your gang. But once married, one needs to keep the spouse informed. A girls' day out or a guys' day out now depends on how comfortable the spouse is with the idea, and whether they want to be a part of it or not.

There also arises the question of friendship with the opposite sex. Is one 'allowed' to have a member of the opposite sex as a friend? If so, will the spouse mind if you meet your friend without the spouse in a coffee shop for a chat? Or will it be seen as the ultimate crime of betrayal? What if it were dinner instead of coffee, or an outing to a pub? Or activities which the spouse does not enjoy, but which the friend does, like watching the IPL finals in the stadium, or going to the Grand Prix? Does one then form a 'guys only' or a 'girls only' gang, as your significant other isn't comfortable with the idea of your going out with members of the opposite sex? Where are the lines drawn and, more importantly, who draws them?

The fact is, you may want to be friends with someone, but your spouse or partner may have nothing in common with them or may dislike them. If one has to constantly ask the spouse for permission to spend time with others, then the one seeking permission would, over a period of time, feel stifled.

As the internet, cell phones and social media become key factors in our lives, couples face newer problems. Does a couple share a password? Or is it better to have a little privacy in your email accounts? A recent study conducted by an internet research project found that 66 per cent of adults who are in a committed relationship or a marriage share passwords. However, a person who fiercely values his/her independence may not want to share passwords. The study also found that 25 per cent of people felt that the phone and internet were a cause of stress in their relationship: they have either discovered messages that they would have rather not seen, or their spouse spends too much time on the internet or on the phone, leaving little room for meaningful conversations between them, which leads to them slowly drifting apart over a period of time.

Sometimes a person who used to be an old flame gets in touch via social media, and if the partner continues to maintain contact with them, no matter how platonic they claim it to be, it could add stress to a relationship, as there has been a certain amount of closeness between them. We have seen how this can affect even the most stable of marriages, in the case of Vish and Shyla in the essay 'On making a relationship last through the years'.

A marriage is between equals. The couple has to set boundaries and decide where their individual freedom ends and where accountability begins, and to what extent should one be accountable. It has to be a joint decision where both are happy to abide by choices made. Placing restrictions on the other person just because you think that is the way they ought to lead their lives would be as ridiculous as expecting your partner to relish fish and chips with gusto just because that happens to be your favourite food.

Whether you decide to get married or not, one thing that cannot be refuted is that a relationship is something that constantly evolves. As individuals, we change and grow over a period of time. If the relationship too evolves, along with the people involved, then it survives the test of time. But if it is subjected to too many factors that stretch it, then it could break down.

And then, sadly, your partner becomes just somebody that you used to know.

The three-year itch in marriages

A FEW YEARS BACK, it was the seven-year itch that caught a marriage by the throat, threatening to choke it. As you became familiar with each other's flaws, the novelty of the relationship wore off and an increased feeling of being trapped set in. You then began to get restless wondering if there was more to a relationship than adjustments and compromises. You also began taking each other for granted and slowly but steadily that wonderful thing called passion got corroded, without either of you realising it, and it was replaced by monotony. And much like a piece of furniture that has been a part of your home for so long that you fail to notice it exists, because you do not really look at it, you both stopped seeing each other the way you used to. Love as the couple knew it slipped away unnoticed and in its place walked a sense of entitlement and 'you belong to me now' all wrapped in the guise of familiarity that slowly bred contempt.

When the movie *Hall Pass* released in the UK in 2011, Warner Brothers commissioned a study to find out when the stress levels in relationships peaked and at what point did boredom set in. What the study discovered was that the earlier seven-year itch had now been shortened to three years, because of the fast-paced nature of life. Amongst the top causes for the passion being killed were weight gain, snoring and stinginess. The pollsters who oversaw the survey said that longer working hours combined with money worries took their toll on relationships, increasing the need for holidays without the spouses and weekends away from home in a desperate bid to carve out breathing space. Couples closeted together for great periods of time needed time alone to recharge their individual batteries and come back to the relationship with renewed vigour.

Dr Helen Fischer, a relationship expert, says that by the third year of living together most couples face a powerful breaking point where the wild, crazy infatuation and initial intense passion that sustained them in the early years wears off. The relationship will last if they discover that they now have an emotional bond. In the absence of that, the bond gets weaker and weaker until it eventually snaps. Dr Fischer says that a trend world over is that if a couple is going to divorce, then it is in the fourth year of marriage where it is likely to happen.

There was another interesting thing that the commissioned study also found: that in the first flushes of romance, the partners received an average of three compliments a week. However, after three years together, this figure fell to a single compliment a week—if at all. It got worse when they lived together longer. Thirty per cent of those who lived together for five years or more said that they never received any compliments from their partners.

So what can a couple do when they find themselves at the mercy of this three-year glitch? Is it all gloom and a downhill ride from now on? Most people regress and behave badly when the relationship falls into troubled waters as they have never really learnt how to handle disappointments in something that used to be source of joy. Some couples drift apart slowly, but some find that they fight more often than they did earlier. Most couples have established a pattern of communication and a pattern of fighting by this point. However, when issues repeatedly do not get resolved and the fights continue, uglier and nastier sides of each other get revealed. The knee-jerk response usually is to flee and escape from the monster that their partner seems to have turned into. But that deals with the issue only temporarily. An approach like that is treating the symptoms, not the cause.

What is needed is to step back from a situation before it explodes. If it has already exploded, then it is best to not act in the immediate aftermath. Give each other space and some time to think things over. Allow the other person to miss you a little bit. Allow yourself to miss the other person and remind yourself of all their good points.

The passion might slowly come back when you begin to look at your partner with new eyes. Sometimes a step backward and a little space might be all a relationship needs to forge ahead with renewed vigour.

How to handle fights in a relationship

My husband recently shared a visual on his Facebook profile that read, 'Don't worry when I fight with you. Worry when I stop as it means there is nothing left for us to fight for.' He felt that it made immense sense if you really thought about it: if there are no fights then it probably means that the couple has slipped into a 'non-caring', passive mode in their relationship. After twenty years of marriage, we still have fights. But the thing is, we make up too. We fight only because we are still passionate enough to care about things that bother us. It means that our love is still alive. It means that we are comfortable enough to express what we want and we aren't afraid of expressing anger towards each other.

Does this imply that those who are experiencing a peaceful relationship have no love left between them? Obviously not. But most couples who have lived together for at least six months would have had a fight at some point or the other. I am yet to come across a couple where every single thing is in sync and harmony, resulting in their navigating the curved and jagged paths of togetherness with the deftness and agility of swimmers in a synchronised swimming event in the Olympics. Once the façade of newness in a relationship has worn thin and familiarity envelops you like a well-worn blanket, the initial niceties are mostly dispensed with, and in creep those little elves called resentment, irritation and annoyance. If neither shows any signs of being affected by it, then they have the patience of a saint and both ought to be canonised, their portraits clicked and framed in the 'perfect relationship hall of fame'. My husband often jokes that if relationships had awards, he should be given a Padmashri for putting up with me for all these years. Instantly, I retort: 'If you get a Padmashri, then I definitely deserve a Bharat Ratna for putting up with you.' After which we always laugh and the tension that has been building up diffuses.

Most couples do form a pattern to their fights. If in one case a partner stomps out angrily, working out his or her frustration in the gym, then in another case the aggrieved partner gives the other the silent treatment, answering their questions or comments with a grunt or an abrupt turn of the face. Then a third kind might take off in the car to drive aimlessly around the city, switching off their mobiles in order to 'teach the other a lesson'. When they have cooled down sufficiently, they may argue, confront and ultimately resolve the issue, or at least bury it till it surfaces again in another form on another day, and the whole cycle gets repeated. No matter how bizarre it may seem to outsiders, each couple develops their own ways to deal with conflicts.

When two people are in a relationship, they are constantly growing and evolving as individuals.

What drew them together in the first place might not necessarily be what is holding them together currently. Each will have their own individual characteristics and quirks which may make no sense to the other person. One of the partners might be the kind that packs a week in advance of a vacation, with air-tickets, passports and everything else photocopied and organised, while the other might be the type who throws in a few clothes into a rucksack at the last minute. Now that by itself might or might not be a cause for conflict, but what it is, is two very different ways of dealing with the same situation. If the relationship is healthy, each partner just lets the other be. But if one of them is controlling—in this case likely to be the super-efficient partner—then there is a chance of a big conflict arising. 'Why do you always pack last minute? Don't you remember when we went last time, you forgot to take the sunscreen and got sunburnt?' might be the attack made, with the other partner retorting that it was not really that big a deal as they managed to buy another sunscreen, whereupon the one who raised it would point out that it was good money wasted which could have been avoided had the packing been done earlier. Thus an issue spirals and snowballs, with more issues being dragged in, till one loses track of what was being argued about to begin with.

Trying to change another person to fit one's own expectations is futile as it will result in resentment on both sides, where the 'corrected party' will feel humiliated and will take offence. After all, nobody likes to constantly hear criticism or be told what to do and how to behave.

If you do want to raise issues, first also appreciate what the other person has done right. For example, in the above scenario, perhaps the partner could first express gratitude and happiness about the fact that the other had made the effort to do all the research for booking the holiday. Then one could word what one felt carefully, in a manner where the tone is non-accusatory. In the above example, the partner could say, 'I feel bad about wasting money on an expenditure that could have been avoided.' When worded that way, there is no accusation, instead an acceptance that it is their own reaction which they are acknowledging. There is no blame and the other partner will probably respond by saying they will remember that the next time.

A healthy relationship would be one that expands and stretches like a sack made of rubber, which would hold everything together—all the quirks, eccentricities, habits and other things that make up our complicated personalities.

The trick is to realise how much the sack can hold.

Can senior citizens find love?

CULTURALLY, INDIANS HAVE BEEN conditioned to believe that once you become a grandparent, your life should revolve around places of worship, prayers and perhaps babysitting coupled with narrating stories to grandchildren. Thinking of love and live-in relationships is something that only the youth does. But what if you are a senior citizen, single and living alone? If you live in India, chances are things like 'finding a partner' will be frowned upon because of the age factor. Most people will dismiss the very idea as preposterous.

However, every now and then, there come along a few incidents or events which break this notion and make us believe that when it comes to finding love, senior citizens are not really at a disadvantage.

The 2007 movie *Cheeni Kum*, directed by R. Balki, tackled wonderfully the issue of prejudice when it comes to elderly folks finding love. In the film, Paresh Rawal personified the 'conventional elderly' in India, while Amitabh Bachchan broke the stereotypes associated with age. In the movie, he plays Buddhadev Gupta, a restaurateur in his sixties who falls in love with Nina (played by Tabu), who is one of his patrons and is in her thirties. Though Buddhadev is older than her dad, the pair decides to go ahead and get married even though they find it very hard to convince others, especially her father, who is against the very thought.

Stories like these infuse, inspire and succeed in reinforcing the fact that age really does not matter. What matters is attitude and courage to really do what your heart tells you to.

A poll of over two thousand people conducted by Age UK, UK's largest charity for older people, reveals that one in eight people aged over sixty-five are seeking companionship. The situation seems to be no different in India. One of the biggest battles that the elderly fight is the problem of loneliness. Their children live abroad or in other cities and are busy pursuing their careers. When one of the partners passes away, the one left behind from a marriage that has lasted for decades suddenly feels lost. Many of them do not like to leave their hometown to move in with their adult children. They are also healthy enough to live independently. Thus arises the need for someone to come home to and spend the rest of their lives with.

In Kerala, three sisters came together and put out a matrimonial advert for their father, a widower, aged seventy. The girls had lost their mother eight years ago, and their father was not willing to move in with any of them. Initially they were very hesitant, wondering if they would get any response at all, but within two weeks, they had over two hundred queries.

Silver Innings, a Mumbai-based initiative to help the elderly lead productive lives, also has a match-making service. At a speed dating event for the elderly organised by them in 2013, six found potential partners and are pursuing relationships, another couple is considering marriage, and four other couples are dating. Silver Innings is run by Kumar Deshpande. When he saw how lonely his father-in-law was after his mother-in-law passed away, Kumar decided to find a match for him. The experience inspired him to organise events for the elderly across various cities.

Thodu Needa, a Hyderabad-based NGO, was started by Rajeshwari, who was around sixty herself then, to help senior citizens find companionship. When she started the organisation in 2010, about forty-five men and twenty-five women attended. A sixty-six-year-old former bank manager and a sixty-three-year-old lady met at this event and decided to live together. Since then Thodu Needa has helped many more people find partners and happiness. Rajeshwari herself, after living alone for more than thirty years, found a match through the organisation, and the wedding was attended by her children as well as her husband's.

Recently, award-winning actor Suhasini Mulay made news when she got married at sixty. She was in a live-in relationship when she was in her forties and eventually that fell apart. She was too busy with her career to find the right man after that, and she continued working, leading a pretty good life as a single woman. Prodded by her friends, she created a Facebook account for her work. She came across a particle physicist online—Atul Gurtu. He had lost his wife to cancer six years earlier. Suhasini was impressed by the article that he had written on her and the two soon started growing closer.

They finally tied the knot, shattering all the stereotypes associated with age, and what is more were accepted by the usually conventional Indian society too.

When Cupid strikes, age ceases to matter. When I was living in the UK, I came across a remarkable love story. During the Second World War, the 617 squadron of RAF, also known as 'The Dambusters', was set up for the specific task of attacking three major dams in Germany. Its accomplishments have now become legend in the annals of military history. Margaret was a very pretty twenty-three-year-old who served with this squadron. Cyril was twenty-two years old when he became a leading air craftsman with the RAF Dutch Spitfire squadron during the same war.

If you think this is a war-time love story, you're wrong. But a love story it is. A remarkable one at that, which demonstrates the endurance of human spirit and that love can indeed strike at any age.

Margaret and Cyril got married a few years ago. Margaret was ninety-three, and Cyril ninety-two. They had met each other five years before at an RAF care home. Neither expected to find love at that stage in their lives, but they did. The *Sunday Express* in Britain carried their story and it quoted Margaret as saying, 'I never thought this would happen again but I love him with all my heart.' Their wedding took place in an eleventh century church in the UK. Both the bride and groom were surrounded by their respective families and RAF airmen.

When I first read their story, I was moved. I admired their courage and their decision. Love can strike at any stage in your life. It might be just around the corner waiting to happen. It might happen when you are at the grocery store picking vegetables, least expecting anything out of the ordinary to occur. It might happen at a parent-teacher meeting. It might happen during a tennis match. It might creep up on you slowly, without you even realising it, and might totally engulf you, sweeping you away, making you a mute spectator to its whims and fancies.

What you decide to do with it is your business. You might let it flourish, or you might brush it aside to pursue whatever it is that you are chasing at that point in your life. You might accept it with open arms or you might refuse to catch it, and it may drop down right beside you and shatter into pieces.

You cannot escape it, this love. It is the driving force of life.

It exists—and if you have it, you are fortunate. If you have found it once and lost it, or if you are still waiting for it, be patient.

Love always knocks again.

WHEN THINGS GO WRONG

Envy, after all, comes from wanting something that isn't yours. But grief comes from losing something you've already had.

–Jodi Picoult

The heart was made to be broken.

–Oscar Wilde

Why break-ups hurt so much

Natasha, a friend who is in her early twenties, came over the other day. She was distraught and holding back her tears. She had just ended it with the man she still loved. They had been in a relationship for three years. She used to call it a yo-yo relationship. At times it was great and there were times it was unbearable. They'd split up before, but had always returned to each other. This time, though, the string had snapped.

'There is a limit to my tolerance. I really think he has commitment issues,' she said when she had settled down a bit.

'I have just the song for you,' I said. I hit play and Gotye began crooning the lyrics of *Somebody That I Used to Know* with a pain so intense that it pierced you, making you stop in your tracks. It was apt for the mood.

'It's too raw for me to listen to right now, but yes, I can relate,' said Natasha.

Somebody That I Used to Know had gone on to hit No. 1 on the Billboard Top 100 in 2012. The fact that the song continues to be extremely popular and is still played on radio channels every so often shows that there are many of us who can relate to its lyrics, having faced the pain of a relationship that didn't work out.

Among all the rejections that we face in life, the one that strikes the hardest and hurts the most is probably when you have been rejected after confessing your love or when a relationship that you were in for a while breaks up. You feel scalded, the physical evidence of which is not visible. Outside, everything seems fine and normal. But inside, you crumble into a million pieces wondering if you will ever be whole again.

I get many letters from young people, writing to me after a break-up, telling me how devastated they are and how much they could relate to characters in my books that are in a similar situation. I understand their pain as the characters I create are mostly based on real-life people who have experienced a hurt similar to theirs. Hence they are able to connect with my fictional characters and, in turn, feel connected to me as I understand the intensity of what they feel.

In a study published in the *New England Journal of Medicine*, scientists demonstrated that they can now objectively measure pain with about 90 to 100 per cent accuracy by studying scans of people's brains. Participants in the study were exposed to multiple levels of heat ranging from mild to bearable to extremely hot, and the images of their brains were studied. The scientists were able to identify a distinct neurological pattern when people are in pain. They then studied the brain activity of people who have been through a break-up and who were shown the image of the person who rejected them. Both the patterns were strikingly similar, proving that the brain activity of someone who was experiencing a break-up was the same as that of someone undergoing acute physical pain. No wonder people have died a natural death caused by heartbreak after a loved one left them.

We also keep reading from time to time about tragic incidents of suicide where, unable to withstand the pain of a break-up, yet another young person has ended their life. That break-ups affect people in ways where they feel they will never be complete again is irrefutable.

The beautiful Nafisa Joseph, a former Miss India, ended her life in July 2004 by hanging herself in her apartment in Mumbai. She was set to marry a businessman in a few weeks but the wedding was called off. She had allegedly been in two relationships earlier that had not worked out for her. A couple of years back, a young techie working in Bangalore was found dead in his car, his face covered with thick plastic and bound with duct tape. The police suspected that it was rejection by a woman—whom he had not even met but only interacted with online, developing an intense relationship through their chats—that drove him to the extreme step. We read of many instances of people ending their lives in the newspapers because a relationship didn't work out. The feelings of heartbreak are intense and those in its grip are engulfed in darkness, pain and hopelessness.

According to the National Crime Records Bureau's 2012 report on accidental deaths and suicides in India, more people in the country end their lives due to heartbreak than unemployment or bankruptcy. Incidents of suicide from love affairs ending badly have increased in the metros, especially Bangalore, Delhi and Mumbai.

The self-diminishing assault of a break-up is extremely hard to endure and every person finds a way to deal with it in a manner that suits him or her best. Some throw themselves into work, take on many new assignments, and immerse themselves in achievable goals, seeking validation that—though their heart is broken—they are still capable of functioning professionally, and doing a darn good job at that. Some drown their sorrows with alcohol—Devdas style—and wish for things that were never meant to be, trying to forget that which is causing them untold misery and pain. Some hit the gym with a vengeance, punishing their bodies, determined to make themselves better, more attractive, fitter, and swearing that never again will they allow anyone to get so close to them. Some call up their friends and cry on whoever will lend them a shoulder. Some, like Adele, make a ballad out of it, top the billboards and go on to earn millions.

I told Natasha that when it came to break-up stories, one of my all-time favourite movies remains *Eternal Sunshine of the Spotless Mind* released in 2004, directed by Michel Gondry. In it, Jim Carrey plays Joel Barish, who is devastated when he discovers that his former girlfriend Clementine, played by Kate Winslet, has undergone a procedure to erase him from her memory. Out of desperation, he contracts the inventor of the process, Dr Howard, to have Clementine removed from his own memory. But as Joel's memories progressively disappear, he begins to rediscover what she meant to him. From deep within the recesses of his brain, Joel attempts to escape the procedure. As Dr Howard and his crew chase him through the maze of his memories, he is astonished to discover that he still very much loves her, and does not want to lose what he cherishes. Though the movie is science-fiction, it touches a deep emotional chord with anyone who has been in a relationship.

'Who knows—maybe I will be the Joel in this relationship,' said Natasha.

Sometimes, no matter how much you try to forget, the heart has its reasons to remember.

How to deal with a broken heart

A FEW WEEKS BACK I received an email from a young man who said he was writing to me in desperation as he did not know how to get over a girl he was madly in love with. She had felt that it wasn't working out with him and he wasn't the guy for her. She had finally broken up with him and she was now married to someone else. Yet, he continued to relive every single memory he had of them together: the things that they had done, the places they had gone, the songs they had dedicated to each other. He fondly recalled the numerous chats they had on instant messengers, all of which he had saved. If there was a soul-mate, she was the one for him, he declared. He doubted if he would ever feel whole again. He felt as though a large part of him was missing, and he sought my advice about what he could do to get over her. He wanted to heal.

A broken heart is a fragile thing. There simply is no quick-fix to heal a broken heart. When you have a fall and twist an ankle, what it needs is rest. You need to rest the foot, not put any weight on it, prop it up, give it hot and cold compress. In time, the body generates new cells and the ankle stops hurting. Heartbreak is like an emotional fall. You cannot see the injuries, but you are hurt. In order to heal, you need to rest. As in the case of the twisted ankle, you wouldn't deny the pain and start walking. If you did, you would risk injuring it further. Similarly, with heartbreak, if you try and pretend that nothing is wrong, you might make things worse in the long run.

There are several things that you can do which can help you to get over that person who is no longer in your life. In order to answer the young man and many like him who struggle with heartbreaks, I put down a five-step plan and, hopefully, it will help.

First step: Acceptance
The first would be to ask oneself if one really wants to move on. Have you accepted that this person and you are never going to have a relationship and you cannot even be friends? Have you decided that you truly want to get over them and move on with your life? This is going to be a very painful process, but if you want to move on, this is one of the things you have to face. And it is going to hurt much more than you can imagine. The pain is going to weigh you down in all that you do. Many people have quit their jobs, dropped out of college and done many things they would never imagine themselves doing because of a break-up. They never thought it would hurt *that* much. The thing about break-ups is that if you want to recover, you have to kill any notion that the person may come back. That part of your life is over. Often we do not realise that we are holding on to false hope.

The very thought of existing without that person in unimaginable. Till now they were a huge part of your life. Now there is going to be a void. In *The Painted Veil,* Somerset Maugham says, 'How can I be reasonable? To me our love was everything and you were my whole life. It is not very pleasant to realise that to you it was only an episode.'

One has to accept the fact that the rest of your life is going to be without them, as hard as that may seem at the moment. Only then is true closure possible.

If you find it very hard to face that or accept that, one of the things that you could do is to write out all that you feel and express yourself completely. Do it as often as you want to. Keep a 'break-up feelings' book if you think that will help. Later, after you have poured your emotions into it, tear up what you have written and bin it. This may sound clichéd but it has helped many. Pouring out your feelings *is* cathartic.

Second step: Axe the sentimentalism

Once you have accepted that they are gone (and this may take several weeks or days depending on how long your relationship lasted), then one has to be ruthless, hard-hearted and determined. Remember, you are trying to reclaim your life. You do not want to keep checking out their photos on social networking sites. So block that person and delete all the old mails, chats, texts and any reminders of the past. Resist all temptation to see what they are up to. The more you stalk on social media, the greater will be the time you take to recover. It is like scratching and opening up a wound that is just beginning to heal. If you are serious about recovery, you have to be serious about sticking to your resolve.

All reminders of them have to go. Fennel Hudson in *Wild Carp* says, 'The things we place greatest value upon are prioritised by their context in our lives.' You have to remind yourself that those things might have been important in the past. But in the current context, they have no place any more. Even the smallest reminder will bring in fresh waves of pain and it will be like starting all over again. You need to set aside half a day and go through all your belongings and search carefully for anything that has to do with them. And then, no matter how expensive it is or what memory it evokes, you have to give it away or bin it. Get rid of the physical reminders.

Third step: Distract yourself
This step is going to be the hardest. The human mind is a monkey that is hard to control. The moment you find your mind wandering to thoughts of them and what they used to say, do and sound like, distract yourself quickly. Show a red light to your mind and ask it to STOP. Hit the gym, go for a walk, do something, but don't think about that person. If you find that hard, allot fifteen minutes in a day to mope, feel sorry, reminisce about them. When the fifteen minutes are over, you are no longer allowed to do any of this. Use a timer if you want! Read a book. Watch a movie. Solve a Sudoku puzzle. Do anything that needs your complete attention. If you find your mind returning to them again and again, start over. It is a constant process needing constant effort on your part. Marcus

Aurelius in *Meditations* says, 'You have power over your mind—not outside events. Realise this and you will find strength.'

Fourth step: Remind yourself that you are loved
Just because that person does not love you, it does not mean you are worthless and your life is going nowhere. Remind yourself of the people who love you—your best friends, your family. Yes, I know it is not the same as that person was truly special. They made you feel like nobody else could. But the fact is you are hurting now. It will help to spend time with positive people who make you laugh. If there is a person who drains you in some way, this is the time to avoid them. Surround yourself with those people who make you feel good about yourself. If you have had relationships before, then think about how you overcame them. If you did it once, you can surely do it again.

Also, remember that there are new people waiting to enter your life. Just like we need to get rid of clutter to physically make space for something on a shelf, so too we need to clear out our minds every now and then to allow room for other people to come in.

Fifth step: Drown yourself in a hobby or a passion
One is spoilt for choice when it comes to recreation these days. Take up your once-forgotten hobby. Join a dance class. Go para-sailing if that is what makes you happy. Do something that you have always wanted to but never did before. Do not wallow, trying to figure out why the relationship did not work. Remind yourself that you are worth more.

How to deal with a broken heart

It may be hard to follow the above initially. But steel yourself and do not waver. Before you know it, you would have reclaimed your life.

These were the things I wanted to tell that young man. But apart from all of the above I also wanted to share with him the story of Oskar Kokoschka, who took his love for his beloved to extreme ends.

Oskar Kokoschka was an Austrian artist, playwright and a poet best known for his intense expressionistic work, the most famous of which is 'The Bride of the Wind', an oil on canvas painted in 1931, currently displayed at Kunstmuseum Basel in Switzerland. It is a self-portrait of the artist lying with his lover Alma Mahler. The painting depicts Alma lying with her head on his shoulder, peacefully asleep, while he stares vacantly into space. Alma met Oskar in 1912; she had been recently widowed and had a four-year-old daughter at the time. Within twenty-four hours of their meeting, they engaged in a passionate love affair. She became his obsession and his life. This uncontrolled, wild passion dominated most of Oskar's works during that period. They all featured Alma. However, their story did not have a happy ending. Kokoschka's intense possessiveness began taking its toll on Alma and the relationship. In 1914, Kokoschka enlisted in the army for the First World War. When he returned, he discovered that Alma had married another man. Oskar was heartbroken. He missed Alma so desperately that he commissioned a skilled mannequin maker, Hermine Moos, to create a life-size replica of her. He provided detailed drawings, sketches and her exact measurements, which he obtained from Alma's dressmaker. Kokoschka wanted the skin to feel sensuous, and so Moos used swan skin for the doll.

Kokoschka used the doll as a model for his paintings, hired nannies to look after it and took it to operas and parties. Newspapers carried stories of this unusual obsession. Finally, at one of the parties, Kokoschka, overcome with emotions, beheaded the doll and poured red wine over it. The following morning the police saw it in Kokoschka's garden and they burst into the house to arrest him, mistaking it for a real human body.

Kokoschka allowed a single obsession to drive him to insanity. He allowed thoughts of Alma to dominate every single thing that he did. Kokoschka could not accept that their relationship had ended, which was why he could not move on and was stuck in a place that tortured him and gave him misery.

What we have to remind ourselves over and over is that relationships happen. But things change. People move on. You feel betrayed, hurt, violated, let down, depressed. Yet there is nothing you can do but go on living, pulling your weary soul behind you. You cannot hold on to something that no longer exists. You have to learn to let go, as hard as it may seem. You have to take one single step at a time. And then go on from day to day. With time, you *will* begin to feel better, no matter how impossible that seems at the moment.

There was so much more that I wanted to tell the young man—to not be so consumed by someone that they have complete control over your emotions. That one needs to get a grip on oneself and believe that, yes, it is possible to survive even the cruellest of cuts and he does not need anybody else to make him feel whole. That he is not alone and many have walked this path before him, and what he is going through is not anything new or unique.

The best thing you can do is to be strong and wait and keep living your life. Remind yourself that with each day that passes you are slowly getting stronger. You are one per cent better than what you were yesterday. The pain will definitely vanish though it doesn't seem like that at the moment. The heart needs time to heal.

How heartbreaks can take lives

A FRIEND AND I were talking about rejection and heartbreak. My friend said, 'The human mind is such a mystery. Why is it that under the same set of circumstances one person snaps and kills 150 people and himself, while another just goes on living his/her life causing no harm to others?'

This was in reference to the German pilot Andreas Lubitz who deliberately crashed the passenger plane he was flying, ending not only his life, but also killing the 150 people on board. It was later reported that he was in a 'relationship crisis' and his personal life was highly troubled.

In another recent tragic incident which took place in Bangalore, an eighteen-year-old girl, Gauthami, was shot dead in her college hostel by the hostel attendant Mahesh. She had allegedly rejected his advances. He also shot another girl, injuring her, and then escaped. He was an errand boy and, on the face of it, he seemed to be a quiet, helpful person. The girl's father went on record stating that Mahesh was a good person and his daughter had never complained about him. He couldn't understand why he had shot her. It is hard to tell what might have gone on in Mahesh's head. But the fact that he was a loner, living in a dark 10'x10' windowless room, with a strong stench of urine and walls plastered with pictures of random women, might be a pointer. Newspaper reports say that mobile phones were banned in the hostel and it was only through Mahesh that the parents could contact the girls.

Both the above incidents reminded me of the Hindi movie *Raanjhanaa,* which deals with an obsessive one-sided love. It is the story of Kundan (played by Dhanush) who falls in love with Zoya (played by Sonam), who is way above his league with regard to education, looks, and standing in society. Zoya is from a family which places an emphasis on education, while Kundan is someone who runs the errands in Zoya's home. What disturbed me about the movie was the alarming regularity with which Kundan would slash his wrists after being told in no uncertain terms by Zoya that her priorities and the love of her life were different from the picture he had painted in his head. Self-destruction was glorified as passion and paraded as all-consuming love.

The difference between a real-life Mahesh, the celluloid Kundan and the airline pilot Lubitz, is that Kundan directed his rage on himself, Mahesh turned it towards the one he was in love with, and Lubitz unleashed it on many innocent people.

Psychiatrists who have analysed the Lubitz case make it clear that depression was not the reason Lubitz killed himself and his passengers. They say that psychiatrists make a distinction between suicide and murder-suicide, the former being self-explanatory and the latter being where the person kills others before killing himself. They assert that the probable reason is that Lubitz had a lot of anger bottled up inside him, as his girlfriend had left him recently and he also had health issues. Lubitz had bought two Audis in an attempt to win her back and had told her that he would leave a mark on the world one day and people would remember him. This rage, combined with loneliness, sadness and inability to cope is what makes people act this way.

Most medical professionals in the field of mental health recommend that the best way to get over heartbreak is to accept the pain, face it and not run away from it. They suggest surrounding oneself with family and friends, exercising, meeting other people and also writing down things that you are grateful for—the things that are going right in your life. I have suggested five steps that will help you recover from a broken heart in the essay, 'How to deal with a broken heart'.

C.S. Lewis had said, 'Love anything and your heart will be wrung and possibly broken. If you want to make sure of keeping it intact you must give it to no one, not even an animal. Wrap it carefully round with hobbies and little luxuries; avoid all entanglements. Lock it up safe in the casket or coffin of your selfishness. But in that casket, safe, dark, motionless, airless, it will change. It will not be broken; it will become unbreakable, impenetrable, irredeemable. To love is to be vulnerable.'

Your current relationship might be the best thing that happened to you and might take you up to giddying heights that you have never been before. It also might plummet you to depths of despair when things go wrong.

And as regards my friend's comment, I told him that the answer lay in the question itself. No two individuals are impacted the exact same way in any situation. In a break-up, the intensity of the pain felt by one is never equal to the intensity of pain felt by another.

It is the way we deal with it that ultimately counts.

How moving homes is like breaking up

MOVING HOMES IS LIKE breaking up. You live in a house for a while, shower love on it, transform it, make some great memories and then when you move, it is all over. All that you are left with is an ache in your heart and a longing for things that can never be.

In the twenty years that I have been married we have moved homes, cities and even countries—the number of times we have moved totals a grand twelve. I know many people who have lived in the same house and the same place their entire life. We moved cities often even when I was a child—and I think I have been richer for it, despite the inconvenience, despite the trouble of uprooting oneself completely and the mayhem that you get thrown into temporarily. I wouldn't have it any other way.

Funny, no matter how many times you move, the process, both physical and mental, remains the same.

There is something about moving home that makes you introspect, makes you think, makes you philosophical and suddenly you see life in a new light. Much like when you end a relationship. The emptiness of the space that used to be home now echoes your voice as all the furniture is gone and only the shell is left. A lot like a relationship where you reflect on the chinks in the armour only when it is over and you are left wondering what happened.

This charged-up wisdom and that quiet acceptance, which I suspect stems from the chaos around you, lasts until the novelty of the new home does or until your newfound perspective settles down too, whichever is earlier, no conditions imposed, no questions asked.

There is the physical stuff to deal with. You do not realise just how much STUFF you have unless you move. I had always prided myself on *not* being a hoarder. I had always prided myself on minimalist living. And then suddenly one realises that there are varying degrees of minimalism too.

Then there are other things you realise. Like the maid that you trusted and who you thought had been doing a good job even when you did not supervise, hasn't really. More than the job not being done well, it is the feeling of being let down that stings you. The feeling of having been taken for a merry ride all this while. You realise how naïve you have been. You realise this at that precise moment when the packers move your sofa and you find a piece of shrivelled-up carrot, a near-empty packet of chips and the lid of a tiffin box which went missing months ago, all staring back at you, almost angrily, their hiding place exposed, as if you have yanked the blanket off a homeless hobo sleeping on the pavement, just to have a look at his face. You turn your eyes away almost guiltily for having discovered this in the first place, and then you move on. Physically.

One of our moves was into a villa in Bangalore, and in true Bangalore (or Bengaluru if you are fastidious) style, the spirit of the entire exercise can be encapsulated in three words: '*Swalpa* adjust *maadi*'—adjust a little. Once the initial 'swalpa adjusting' was dealt with, things began slowly settling down like mud that gets plastered to the ground in a heavy downpour. It is indeed uncomfortable when it rains, save for those times when everything is perfect in your life and you watch it safely from your window, *dry,* sipping your tea and having pakodas.

When we arrive at our villa, the one we are moving into, the carpenters are still working at a cabinet in the kitchen, despite having assured us that everything will be ready well in time. The floor is completely wet—a last-minute bid to clean up the villa before we arrived. The workers have poured buckets of water on the floor and then, when the moving truck arrives, realise that there is no way you can navigate a wet floor carrying a forty-six-inch Sony Bravia TV. Enlightened with this realisation, they scuttle and spring into action and the person in charge hurriedly sends out his people to *buy* mops.

I go back to my old house and supervise the truck being loaded, telling them to do it slowly as the house we are shifting into is just getting ready. By noon, the spouse makes a frantic call to me. I make a frantic call to the guy who assured me it would all be done well in time. He assures me again that the villa will be ready to move into in an hour. When it is in fact ready, the time is seven-fifty in the evening. And the work is not really over. But I have *swalpa adjust maadi-ed* and moved in lock, stock and barrel—okay, make that husband, two kids, a large, active Doberman and hundreds of boxes full of stuff.

The poor packers and movers have worked really hard and, by the time they leave, it is eight-thirty in the evening. My poor dog (my third baby, although others see her as a fierce Doberman), has been locked up in her crate the whole day, watching all this stuff happening, and seeing so many people handling HER family's stuff has upset her no end. It is pure torture for her as her instinct is to guard and be fiercely protective. She would be happy to take a nip or two of the workers' bottoms but I do not think that is part of the contract and so we have a really hard time controlling her.

Now we are in our new home surrounded by cardboard boxes—the accumulation of sixteen years of togetherness, our memories, things which matter, some which don't, all boxed in, neatly labelled, easily moved. If only we could do that with our relationships in life.

All that is left to be done now is to unpack.

And at that moment, it feels like I am going to be busy doing just that for the next 365 days. Much like a break-up, the recovery is going to be slow, painful, laborious, lengthy. I know I am going to miss my old home.

But sometimes life gives you no other option but to move on.

ON MEN AND WOMEN

Men are from Earth, women are from Earth. Deal with it.

–George Carlin

Why women love high heels

It was that kind of idyllic day where the weather was perfect, neither too hot nor too cold, and a mood of joyful mellowness had enveloped the city like a fluffy blanket, comforting our souls. Naina and I were sitting on the rooftop of a posh restaurant, sipping our margaritas, talking about life in general (mine) and men in particular (hers). The conversation then turned to all matters sartorial and she asked me in a conspiratorial whisper how many pairs of heels I owned. 'Three six-inch ones, one four-inch one and a couple of flats,' I answered truthfully, whereupon she had to suppress a scream of disbelief proclaiming that I must be abnormal or the only woman on Earth to own so *few* shoes.

'Why, how many do you own?' I asked.

She had to admit that it was more than a hundred and thirty, whereupon it was my turn to gasp.

'My boyfriend never understands how I can walk in some of them,' she said sheepishly.

'True that,' I nodded. 'A man will never get what it is.'

And I was talking not just about the obsession with heels, I was also talking about the other thing that high heels involve—true pain.

If you are a man, chances are you do not know what true pain is. Not the emotional, gut-wrenching, she-chopped-off-my-testicles kind of a pain that you experience when the woman you are in love with drops you faster than a McLaren F1 which, after leading for most rounds showing promise of winning the Grand Prix, turns turtle and crashes, but the very real physical pain that comes from wearing high-heels, which most women have been privy to at some point of time or another. Whether they decided to embrace the pain, made peace with it or ditched it completely for more comfortable, flatter protection for their soles is another footwear story.

But a few brave men have gone ahead and experienced what it feels like to wear high heels. Images of these men walking in women's shoes in striking psychedelic colours such as red, electric blue and even canary yellow made waves in Nottingham, UK recently. A similar set of pictures also made the rounds in July 2013, in Dongguan, China, where a group of men paraded through an amusement park wearing women's heels.

No, these were not cases of men with a fetish for women's shoes, deciding to expose the secret cross-dressing fantasies that they have long nurtured and till now carefully shielded from society's prying eyes lest they be jeered at for being different. The exercise was part of an event organised by a charity to raise awareness about domestic violence against women.

Similar events have been held in various cities all across the world at different points in time under a programme called 'Walk a mile in her shoes', which encourages men to walk a mile wearing high heels.

When men walk in women's shoes (literally, not just metaphorically), they experience what their partners, be it girlfriend, wife, mistress, want-to-be-mistress, or their married secret lovers, go through. Would it make them more empathetic towards women and their problems? That remains to be discovered, but it is sure to make them think once they are done nursing their blisters, bunions and sore feet, an unwelcome gift from the not-so-friendly women's heels, which their one-mile walk is certain to have produced.

For the record, 2.5 inches is a 'low heel', one that is between 2.5 and 3.5 inches is considered a mid-heel, and anything higher than that is a true-blue high heel guaranteed to evoke drool, much like the fabled deodorants that promise to get you laid.

For many decades now, a woman in heels has been considered sexier and more attractive than one in a pair of flats. What is it about a woman in heels that makes men take a second glance, if not make them go weak in the knees?

High heels are a powerful instrument of seduction. Who can forget the kinky scene in *The Wolf of Wall Street* where Margot Robbie pushes her stilettos into a grovelling Leonardo DiCaprio's face? The same scene with flat footwear wouldn't have had quite the same impact.

It is a known fact that high heels accentuate a woman's femininity, altering the gait as the wearer is forced to take short strides and quicker steps. The legs appear elongated and natural curves are accentuated, thus increasing the wow-look-at-her quotient. It is a very primal instinct—after all a woman in high-heels cannot run very fast—that excites men.

Also, do not discount the fact that a woman in very high heels could play the damsel-in-distress-caused-by-high-heels card and ask a guy to lend her his arm while walking, a gesture that would make any man feel more macho than Indiana Jones in the temple of doom, completely giving vent to the protector/caregiver role of the caveman days, in a socially acceptable manner, with no eyebrows raised.

And no matter how much the osteopathic studies shout from the rooftops that high-heels are bad for your back, your ankles, your posture, your health in general, and your wallet in particular, the sale of high heels have only increased, clearly indicating that women love their heels as much as—or to be scathingly honest, perhaps a teeny-weeny bit less than—they love their men.

And whether the men in their lives stay or not, a woman's high heels will be with her forever.

Is casual sex worth the effort?

IF SOMEONE FROM THE eighteenth century were to travel to the present era, like the character that Hugh Jackman plays in the 2001 romantic starrer *Kate & Leopold*—also featuring Meg Ryan—he would scratch his head in puzzlement. He would be astonished not only at the gigantic progress made in all fields ranging from science and technology to architecture, transport, medicine and many more, but also at the societal changes that have taken place, right from the way we connect to the way we socialise, interact with others and go about our daily lives.

If, in his era, women left the chasing in the dating-mating scene to men, in the current scenario he would find no such distinction. He would find a sexually more permissible society and would be stupefied at the several apps that help people find others in the same locality who are interested in a no-strings attached sexual encounter. Casual sex, friends with benefits and booty-calls are all by-products of the times we live in. A booty call is a call or a text made by one party to another for sex that day, while 'friends with benefits' is people who remain friends while having sex with each other, with no plans of getting into a relationship.

While things like these were unheard of in India about fifty years back, the attitude today is far more relaxed when it comes to casual sex. A group of us women were meeting after a while and catching up on each other's lives. We were all single at that time and this was before the advent of smartphones and the internet. One woman in our group was inconsolable, just having been dumped by a guy she was sure she would be getting married to.

'You know what, you should just go and sleep with someone. The best way to get over somebody is to get under somebody,' said someone in the group, and we all laughed.

'I can't go through all the motions needed for that. It's just too much trouble,' replied the distraught woman.

Even as little as ten years back, when someone wanted to have casual sex, their best bet was the local bar or the pub, where hopeful singles with similar thoughts thronged. There used to be flirting, buying a drink for the lady, exchanging compliments, getting slowly drunk, as everyone and everything around faded out gradually and the object of your interest grew more attractive with each passing hour, and finally the question, 'Your place or mine?', was popped, a graceful exit made and, hailing a cab discreetly, the couple headed away for a night of unbridled passion, laced with the thrill of the chase that led to the final encounter. Hooking up was an art honed, practised and unhurried.

But the smartphone came along and changed all that. It waved its magic wand turning us all into instant-gratification junkies. It eroded our patience, ate away social skills like flirting, making small talk and eye contact. We now click photos of brilliant sunsets with our high megapixel smartphone cameras and, rather than savouring the moment and enjoying the view of the sun going down, we get busy uploading it to Instagram, quickly checking who liked it and how many hearts it managed to get. Friendships are instant too, for we connect with people across the globe as we read their blogs and discover an intimacy of the mind, establishing a connection even if we have never set eyes on that person. It is possible to create friendships through the mouse without budging from home.

Everything that we desire is delivered instantly, with just a click. Even sex.

There are several apps that have been developed for casual sex on demand. You can download these apps on your phone and they offer a connection to people who are looking for casual hook-ups and no-strings-attached sex. An app like Blendr asks to link to your Facebook to access location, photos and interests. Other users who have downloaded it are shown too. You can look for similar-minded people in your area and then hook up. There are other apps where the user can stay anonymous and 'wink' at people who have downloaded the app. If a response is received and interest is expressed, the user can then choose to reveal more details. Then there are others where you can connect only with the friends on your list who are looking for a one-night stand. You can browse through photos and choose the person you are interested in. If that person too chooses you, then you get a notification, and the rest is up to the individuals involved.

Experts agree that apps like these are popular as it is easier to shed one's inhibitions online. The fear of rejection, which is very much there when you approach someone in a bar, gets reduced greatly when you use an online app, where nobody will even know whether you have tried to 'get lucky' or not. Users of this app will naturally put up only their best photos and embellish other details to sound smart, savvy and attractive. The emphasis here is on looking attractive enough to hook someone. As shallow as it may be, the 'results' are quick and instant.

But, hooking up via apps such as these come with inherent dangers and one should take precautions, for instance, letting a trusted friend know where you're going. The very medium, because of its anonymity, means that you never know what kind of a person you might be connecting with.

Also one needs to take into account the repercussions that casual sex can have. As much as we like to believe that we will dust off our emotional antennae and walk away unscathed, there is a possibility that one can get singed too. Much like potato chips, which feel so good while you're eating them but leave you with extra calories and a 'why in the world did I eat so much' feeling, casual sex too can come with after-effects that you did not foresee. I know of people who have done it in the heat of the moment and later regretted it immensely, and I also know people who have used it in order to get over heartbreak, the loss of a pet or a job. And needless to say, apart from the emotional repercussions, it is always wise to use precaution rather than get carried away by passion as the risk of STD or an unwanted pregnancy is always there.

In a study published in *Human Nature*, which sought to test the commonly-held stereotypical belief that men are more interested in sex than women, it was found that men have much lower standards than women when it came to one-night stands. In a social science experiment conducted in Florida University, the researchers sent out people as 'predators' or 'baits'. They instructed them to approach strangers that they considered attractive enough to sleep with and to strike up a conversation to see if they would agree to a date, a trip back to the 'predator's' apartment or a casual sexual encounter. None of the women approached agreed to casual sex and 3 per cent agreed to a trip back to the apartment. However an astonishing 75 per cent of the men approached agreed to sleep with the 'predator', no matter if they were good-looking or not.

In another study published in 2008, in a journal of Durham University, it was discovered that most women reported negative feelings and a feeling of 'being used' after a one-night stand, even though it was completely consensual. They also felt they had let themselves down and were worried about their reputation if other people found out. The study seems to indicate that, when it comes to casual sex, men and women are wired differently and most women do experience some amount of negativity and guilt.

Evolutionary psychologists have explained over and over that men are programmed to spread their seeds—

hence have sex with as many women as possible—but it is now found that monogamy may be as problematic for women as it is for men. A growing body of research indicates that the attitudes of women are changing, along with the times.

Daniel Bergner in his book *What Do Women Want: Adventures in the Science of Female Desire* questions the theories in the earlier studies. What Bergner says is that when the social stigma with a one-night stand is stripped off and the possibility of physical danger in a casual sexual encounter is taken away, then women say yes to casual sex just as often as men. Bergner, in his numerous visits to primatologists, found that female monkeys are much more sexually aggressive than males and it was the same with rodents. He suggests that this could do with the fact that society and general conditioning is such that we are all more accepting of male sexual initiation, thus perpetrating stereotypes. In an experiment with speed-dating, when gender norms were reversed—men remained seated while women made the rounds—it was found that women were ticking as many boxes as men usually did.

In the light of the above findings, Billy Crystal's statement that, 'Women need a reason to have sex. Men just need a place', might no longer be true. All women need, apart from a place, could probably be an attractive man, who treats them right.

When it comes to casual sex in the Indian scenario, a quick glance at my Facebook feed shows me that the twenty-somethings are pretty open about their relationships. A young girl posts a list of all the things that turn her on. Another young man writes a lengthy post on how he doesn't really care about whether a girl's skirt is short or not and whether she is a virgin or not or even how many sexual partners she has had. A third posts his experience with Tinder and how unsuccessful he has been at finding a woman for casual sex and how it made him feel like a failure. Casual sex is no longer a taboo subject.

However, many young girls feel that it is not worth the trouble as one has to deal with the emotional aftermath. Samyukta, twenty-four, works in a multinational corporation and shares a flat with two other girls. She says that while her flatmates swear by casual sex, she really is not into it. She says she will never have casual sex with someone she is not comfortable with and someone she doesn't trust, not because she is a prude but because she feels it may not be worth the effort. If she is comfortable with the guy, he is discreet, and she is sure that he will not go around telling others that he 'scored with her', then she may consider it. But she is yet to find that guy to have casual sex with!

Anandita, twenty-one, who is in her final year of college, feels that it all looks great in the movies where a young girl goes out on her own, picks up a guy and ends up having great sex with him. In real life, it hardly works out that way. She did try it once and she hated it. She felt lousy for many days afterwards and finally had to speak to a counsellor to sort out her emotions. She is now convinced that in order to have good sex you have to know each other really well, and only when you have a certain level of comfort around each other is that possible. She says that she doesn't look at sex merely as a physical need to be taken care of.

Twenty-two-year-old Pratyush feels one-night stands are a great idea as there is no commitment on either side, and you can just have a wild time and forget about it the next morning. He likes the fact that you may never see the person again. When asked about the possibility of sexually transmitted diseases, he says that is a cause for concern, which is why he always uses protection.

The thing to remember before you jump into a casual sex encounter is that there are definitely bound to be feelings involved sooner or later. Whether the pain which will come later is worth enduring for the instant pleasure which a casual sex encounter may or may not provide is a choice that you have to make. You may jump in with gusto and discover that you don't like it after all.

But to escape unscathed will be harder than you imagine.

Is it worth the risk or not: this is for people to decide for themselves. And as long as both parties are adults, know what they are doing and want to go ahead with the perceived thrill that casual sex with a stranger provides, then the apps provide just the opportunity.

Whether or not there is a happy ending to it—your guess is as good as mine!

Is friends-with-benefits a good option in relationships?

IF YOU WERE A young man living in Europe in the 1800s and you fancied a woman, you would have to call on her parents and express your interest. Her parents would then permit you to talk to her and get to know her. All this would be without sex or physical contact ever entering the picture. Many families from lower income groups had small homes and couldn't accommodate the prospective suitor, hence the couple began leaving the house, with the parents' permission, to spend some time together. This is how the phrase 'going on a date' came into existence and got popularised.

But people went on these dates only if there was an interest to get married. The initial date was a meeting to whet out similarities, find out more about the other person and to see if they liked each other enough to spend the rest of their lives together.

This began changing in the mid-Sixties. With the invention of the birth control pill, a sexual revolution began. People began to have more sexual encounters.

The dating era slowly metamorphosed into a 'hook-up' culture. The idea that women were entitled to their sexual pleasure as much as men took root and spread rapidly. People became more in tune with their sexuality and inner desires. The way we had sex changed. The sexual revolution that originated in the West came to India too, and today in the Indian metros, going on dates, hooking up and one-night stands are very common.

A curious by-product of this sexual liberation is something that has sprung up in very recent times: the 'friends-with-benefits' scenario. 'Friends with benefits' is a situation where two friends have sex on a regular basis. It may or may not develop into a romantic relationship. It is a relationship which also has the friendship element and it's not an association purely for sex, like a one-night stand. It is likely to be kept a secret or might be known only to a few close friends. It is not a relationship that one would flaunt on a social networking site or even mention to the family. It may be short-lived, with both parties moving when their circumstances change.

Vaibhav, twenty-eight, a techie, had a 'friends-with-benefits' relationship with Maya when he was in his final year of college. Maya was in his college, but in a different stream, and she shared a flat with three other girls. Vaibhav and Maya really enjoyed each other's company and were great pals. If anything good happened to Maya, the first person she would share the news with was Vaibhav. It was the same for him. All their friends were more or less certain that they would end up with each other, even though both vehemently denied it and said that they weren't anything more than good friends. The sex was great and both were really happy for a while. They both finished college and began working. The arrangement continued, but while it suited Vaibhav just fine, Maya started wanting more from it. She became possessive about him and started acting like his girlfriend, at which point he broke off from her. It was very hard for him as she persisted, kept following up with him, trying to make things better, and he harboured feelings of guilt for a long time afterwards. He still feels bad about losing a great friend and misses her, but there is no going back. For him that door is closed. Maya too eventually moved on and is now married.

The 'friends-with-benefits' kind of relationship, a reflection of the times we live in, has attracted the attention of social scientists as well as filmmakers.The 2011 movie *No Strings Attached,* which stars Natalie Portman and Ashton Kutcher, is a story on this theme where a guy and a girl try their best to have just a physical relationship but learn how hard it is. The movie *Friends with Benefits*, released the same year, starring Mila Kunis and Justin Timberlake, deals with two young people who discover that adding sex to a lovely friendship can indeed complicate things.

However, contrary to popular belief or what is depicted in the movies—that adding sex to a relationship might just ruin it—a recent study conducted in November 2013, published in *The Archives of Sexual Behaviour*, discovered that 80 per cent of the participants had had a friends-with-benefits relationship with someone and continued to remain good friends even when the sex ended. Fifty per cent of the participants reported feeling closer to their friend once they had sex with them. Only 18.5 per cent of the participants did not remain friends.

So how do friends-with-benefits relationships end? Much like friendships, which are dynamic and change according to the situations that people find themselves in, this relationship too undergoes changes. One of the parties might fall in love with someone else and might not want to continue the sex. The sex itself might be bad and they may discover that they are not sexually compatible. Boredom might creep in, just like it does in a marriage, and in the absence of commitment, one of them may decide to end it like in the case of Vaibhav and Maya.

But if the sex is good, and if the friendship becomes stronger, then one might just have a perfect Hollywood ending, where the guy gets the girl and they walk off into the sunset, their hearts dancing in wild abandon at having found the perfect relationship—where you marry a very good friend who understands you perfectly and as a cherry on the cake, is great in bed too.

Why watches are male and keys are female

YEARS AGO, WHEN I was single, if you had talked to me about the importance of organising a space and keeping things where they belong, I would have automatically categorised you as 'those older people' kinds. You would think that, now that I have my own children and a home to run, I would endorse the actions of *those older people,* but you would be wrong. I am older and wiser and I know some things with greater certainty now that I didn't twenty years back. Also the experience that I gained has helped me to develop my own theories now on many things, like parenting, running a home, friendships, relationships, marriage, financial independence, gender equality and such. I also have a theory about the kinds of people that inhabit our planet Earth.

I believe there are two kinds of people in the world: those who always know where their keys are kept and those who spend at least ten minutes every day looking for them. No prizes for guessing which category I fall into—the second undoubtedly. (Another theory that I now believe in is that becoming a parent does not change your basic nature. It just gives you an excuse to be disorganised. 'What? I don't have time for all that—I have kids and a home to run.' I also don my writer hat and throw around vague statements like, 'I can't be bothered about mundane things like keys. I have a story plot running in my head.') I spend time looking for my keys *every single day*. It is a ritual now. 'Baby, have you seen my keys?' I utter that statement with the frequency with which newlyweds say 'I love you' to each other.

In addition to keys, I also spend time looking for my watch and sometimes my earrings too. I am now convinced that these things come alive at night, much like the creatures in *Night at the Museum*. If you do not agree with me, I suggest you keep a night vigil. And be very alert. If you are quiet enough, you can hear the watch tell the keys, 'Hey, let's have some fun tonight—where do you want to go?' Keys can open doors, and with watches time is really not an issue, so they wander off, God knows where, through open windows or closed doors and have a great time. (I assume they have a good time, else they would come back, wouldn't they?) So that leaves me with just one option—to launch a massive search operation for them.

Presuming that I began using my own keys at the age of sixteen, and considering that on an average I spend ten minutes every day looking for them, I have spent 98,550 minutes so far just hunting for my keys! Add to it another ten minutes looking for my watch and earrings and the figure doubles. Ms Keys and Mr Watch are never found together, you know.

In case you want to know what makes me so sure that keys are a Ms and watches are a Mr, I have a theory for that too. I am a staunch believer in the saying, 'Good girls go to heaven but bad girls go everywhere'. So Ms Keys is definitely a bad girl. As for the watch, it has to be a 'Mr' because, like most men when you go looking for them, is found either on the bed, sofa or in the bathroom. The watch is also relatively easier to find than keys—blame it on the deviousness of the female of the species—and is usually content perching on the sofa, in front of the television.

Ms Keys, on the other hand, has turned up in the oddest of places. One time she was discovered in the garbage bin, chatting with potato peels and garlic skin. Fortunately this was in the evening and the garbage hadn't been placed outside. Another time, Ms Keys was found inside the washing machine, happily ensconced in the pocket of my jeans. She was discovered only after the whole wash cycle had been completed. It was just as well, because the soap and water worked wonders and she looked sparkly clean. I don't think she was satisfied with the wash I had given her in the kitchen sink, after her unceremonious retrieval from her cosy tête-à-tête with the garbage bin. Another time she was found chilling inside the refrigerator. I definitely hadn't sent her there. My theory is that she wanted to taste the leftover Chinese takeaway that I had put away the previous night. Yet another time, she was found in the footwear rack, nestling between a pair of stilettos and crocs. Now why would she do that, tell me? I am quite sure it was a diabolical plot to ensure that I was a prisoner in my own house while my friends, after waiting for me for the fifteen minutes that I hunted for her (having retrieved my sneakers from the same footwear rack, mind you), finally gave up and went for a walk without me.

Do you know where she was found once? You'd never guess: she was on the keyboard of the home computer. The keyboard is on a sliding shelf that has been pushed in. So *these* keys and *those* keys were having a cosy time, you see, till the children came home in the evening, discovered them, and yelled, 'Mummy—we found your keys.'

Yet another time, all of us spent almost half an hour looking for the keys. Husband, children, house help and the dog were roped in for the 'Great Indian Key Hunt'. Guess where we finally found them? It was the last place that I'd think of looking—on the key holder on the wall, where they're supposed to be!

Ms Keys has also been found in the dashboard of the car, in a spectacle case, inside the toy cupboard, on the rocking chair in the garden, on top of the microwave in the kitchen, on the treadmill, on the bean bag, inside the liquor cabinet and, one time, even in the local grocery store.

Like I was telling you, good girls go to heaven but bad girls go everywhere. My keys—they are bad. Definitely bad. Outright evil, wicked, at times bordering on cruel and sadistic.

But the thing is—like all bad girls—she eventually comes back. And dear Ms Keys, I forgive you because of that basic rule on which all relationships thrive: I need you more than you need me.

Why flirting is good for you

FLIRTING IS A NATURAL human instinct, just like hunger, thirst and the urge for sex. Not only is it universal and common across all cultures and countries, but it is also an integral part of human interaction. According to evolutionary psychologists, flirting is essential as it is a courtship device, without which the human race would not have progressed to reproduction. We are genetically programmed to flirt.

Sometimes it is done subconsciously: research shows that 55 per cent of flirting is done through body language, 38 per cent is through the tone of our voice and only a mere 7 per cent is through what we say. Thus an innocuous thing like, 'Pass me the butter', can be the ultimate seduction weapon, based on how one says it and where and in what tone.

Most of us recognise flirting when we encounter it. It can be verbal: teasing, challenging someone intellectually or paying them compliments. It can be physical, like looking into the eyes, looking away and looking back again, a warm smile, a light touch on the arms, a toss of the hair or challenging them in a sport.

It can be through emails or text messages peppered liberally with emoticons. It can even be a direct declaration with an outrageous statement like, 'Oh, now that I have seen you, I know my day is going to be great.' It will be hard to find a person who is not pleased when someone flirts with them, as it is an affirmation that the person finds you attractive—irrespective of the relationship status of the participants.

Every flirtatious activity does not mean that the person wants it to lead to sex. Studies have shown that many people flirt without any intention of having sex, but simply because they enjoy it and it boosts their self-esteem, and also because flirting opens doors, sometimes leading to great friendships.

Some psychologists say that flirting may even help improve marriages, helping to add that extra zing to it, as long as the foundation of love is strong between both partners. A man might see someone else flirting with his wife at a party, and if she were to flirt back, he would see her not just as the mother of his children and his wife, but as an attractive woman in her own right, whom he should not take for granted. A woman who has not been paying much attention to her husband might find her interest suddenly piqued when she sees that other women want him.

The thing about flirting is what is construed as crossing a line. The boundaries that you define for yourself might be different from that which the other person has in mind. If a guy consistently flirts with a woman who is not interested, she could perhaps raise hell about sexual harassment. If a woman flirts with a married man and his wife does not like it, she can be sure that she will never again get invited to their home. Thus a remark such as, 'You look beautiful', can be misread as it hinges on the border of being a compliment or being a pass, depending on what the person perceives as 'okay' or 'not okay'.

In a study conducted in Northern Illinois University, it was found that men were worse than women when it came to reading verbal clues and body language. Men often overestimated the woman's interest in them and wrongly interpreted flirtatious behaviour as more sexual than intended. It was also found that when women flirted in a sexually suggestive way, men found them more attractive. But the men who flirted this way were seen as pushy and less attractive.

In the end, a relationship is between two individuals. What is okay for a couple might be taboo for another. Flirting can be fun, infectious and an inexpensive pick-me-up on a lousy day. But if either of the parties is not comfortable or crosses that invisible line, then it can also spell disaster.

The trick is to be able to tell when it is okay to flirt, with whom and to what extent. What is sauce for the goose is clearly not sauce for the gander.

How cuddling helps a relationship

IN THE 2014 BOLLYWOOD movie *Finding Fanny*—a movie I loved—Angie (Deepika Padukone) tells Savio (Arjun Kapoor) that instead of a post-coital cuddle, she would prefer rolling over and smoking a cigarette had she been a smoker, thereby making a statement. They do not cuddle like couples usually do after sex and she spends the rest of the night gazing at the stars. This is in direct contrast to what surveys tell us—that the worst thing that a guy can do after sex is roll over and go to sleep, instead of cuddling the woman, hugging her and telling her that she is great or beautiful—whichever is applicable. Angie is perhaps an exception rather than the rule as most people would prefer some kind of contact after the act.

A study from Indiana University has revealed that cuddling, hugging and caressing are very important for satisfaction when it comes to a long-term relationship. The international study analysed over a thousand couples from different countries, including the US, Brazil, Germany, Japan and Spain. They had been together for an average of twenty-five years or more. They reviewed the levels of sexual satisfaction as well as happiness in the relationship. Surprisingly, tenderness was more important to men than women. It was also discovered that men and women reported a higher sexual satisfaction if there was more cuddling and kissing in the relationship.

Science and evolutionary scientists have demonstrated through several studies and experiments that the need for physical contact is a very important part of our species heritage. All primate babies cry, suckle and cling—behaviour that promotes physical proximity with the caregivers, helping the babies survive. All of us have a deep and inherent need to be held, cuddled.

The need for a cuddle, just like the need for sex, is so basic and deep-rooted that people are finding innovative ways to fulfil it. In Japan, there is a 'cuddle café' called Soineya, which offers clients the opportunity to cuddle and sleep with another person for about six thousand yen an hour. There is no sex involved and sexual contact is strictly prohibited. One basically goes there to fall asleep in the arms of a stranger, who cuddles you—at a price, of course.

In Portland, US, Samantha Hess is a professional cuddler. She cuddles people for about sixty dollars an hour. Sex is strictly prohibited and the clients have to keep their clothes on. They also have to sign a waiver before a session, promising to be clean and courteous. The services offered are strictly platonic and she requires that each person meets her in a public place so they can sit down, chat and get to know each other a little more before they cuddle. The cuddle sessions she offers are usually in the clients' homes, parks or in a movie theatre. Jackie Samuel, who is based in Penfield, New York, also offers cuddle sessions for one dollar a minute. She has named her business 'The Snuggery', and she launched a company officially when she was doing her Masters in Social Work at the University of Rochester. She says that though sexual arousal can happen, and sometimes does, during a cuddle session, it is normal, but no sex or nudity is allowed. Jackie says that if she has a steady income, then she would love to provide cuddles to homeless people and people who are isolated from society. Ali C. is another woman in New York who cuddles for money and she has a variety of packages, like the two hundred-dollar movie package or the five hundred-dollar overnight cuddle package to choose from.

As I write this, I can't help reflecting. I feel blessed to have people in my life who love me unconditionally, who comfort me when I am sad, who listen when I want to talk to someone, and who physically hug me, cuddle me and hold my hand.

We live in extremely hard times, where people are connected socially but have less and less time for others. Loneliness is woven into the very fabric of our existence. And the very fact that there are businesses that thrive on cuddles shows that there are many extremely lonely people in the world who just want to be held.

Even if they have to pay for it.

What makes you a bad girl in India?

A FEW MONTHS AGO I came across a well-educated, well-travelled woman who, at the insistence of her husband, wore a saree at home with the *pallu* over her head in the presence of his parents. Apparently his parents wanted a 'good daughter-in-law' and he did not want them to feel upset about a 'modern wife'. The deal between them was that when they went out alone, she could wear whatever she pleased. The funny thing is that I seemed to be the only one who found this arrangement shocking. The lady was very comfortable with it.

'Don't you mind doing it? I mean don't you want to wear something that you would like to instead of being forced to comply?' I couldn't resist asking.

'It's a small thing he is asking of me. He does everything for the house. He just wants to please his parents,' she replied.

She later told me that her husband took care of everything financially and she was blessed to be married to him; she considered herself fortunate. What can one say when it is a choice deliberately made? If she was okay with it, who was I to judge?

It reminded me of the poster of a 'bad girl' that made the rounds on the internet and generated equal amounts of laughter and disgust. It finally turned out to be a satirical one. The poster was composed by a group of students of a design school in Bangalore, who were asked to juxtapose images from popular culture as part of an assignment. They created the 'bad girl' poster in the style of the 'ideal boy' posters that used to be popular in the Eighties, taking their cue from the hugely popular spoof of these posters by artist Priyesh Trivedi, which showed the ideal boy wreaking mayhem wherever he went. They never expected the poster to gain the momentum that it did.

The original 'ideal boy' posters, put up in primary schools in the Eighties, attempted to mould boys—though I fail to understand why they did not include girls in this—into good, honest, kind, peace-loving and helpful men. It had pictures with a caption underneath, suggesting the activities that an ideal boy should do. They included things like getting up early in the morning, saluting parents, going for a walk, brushing teeth, bathing daily, praying, going to school and reading attentively, helping others, eating meals on time, taking lost children to the police station and participating in social activities. It made you wonder whether children were regularly getting lost in India in the Eighties. In the brilliantly executed spoofs, the ideal boy is shown doing various things including smoking weed. I particularly liked the one which showed the ideal boy on the left, holding a glass jar full of currency notes with the caption saying 'Tipping is not just a country in China'; on the right, it had the

Hindi alphabet, with the name of a popular rock band for each letter. *Dha se* Doors, *Pa se* Pink Floyd, etc.

In the 'bad girl' poster that went viral, the 'bad girl' smoked and drank, went to Goa, watched porn, walked outside with 'hair open', ate too little, fell in love in a park and rode a motorbike.

After Leslie Udwin's controversial documentary *India's Daughter* was banned, another 'bad girl' satirical chart started doing the rounds on the internet. This one was called 'Bad girl in the eyes of a rapist'. Here the 'bad girl' roamed around after nine o'clock at night, spoke in English, went to a pub and a disco, did not do housework (instead she is shown painting a picture on a canvas), worked at night, went out with boys, filed an FIR and resisted the rapist.

Sadly all of these struck a chord. Satire has often been used to highlight issues that are grave, gruesome and dark. Will these posters change minds steeped in patriarchy? Perhaps not. But what they do is give vent to pent-up frustration and sheer helplessness in situations that we do not have any control over.

Many of my women friends gleefully declared that they are bad girls after the posters did the rounds. They agreed with me that good girls went to heaven, but bad girls went everywhere. And then we planned a ladies' night out.

We made sure to get one of our drivers though, to drive us home safely. We didn't want to 'invite trouble'. You can be as bad as you like, but when it comes to getting back safely, better get someone trustworthy to drive you home.

This is India after all.

Why space is important in a relationship

'I JUST NEED SOME space,' said Sanjay as he stormed out of the house, banging the door shut, leaving behind a very bewildered Tanuja. All she had done was ask Sanjay if he would accompany her to choose a saree to gift her mother. He had asked her to go by herself but she had insisted that he come with her.

Sanjay and Tanuja had been married for three years and did not have any children. Both held high-paying jobs in software companies and had had fights and made up, but this was the first time that Sanjay had done something so drastic. Tanuja just couldn't understand what Sanjay meant when he said 'I need space'. After all, both were at work almost the whole day through the week and saw each other only late in the evenings. Their weekends were always spent together though. Since Tanuja's parents lived in the same town, they would often visit them. At times they went out with common friends. There wasn't a single activity that they did by themselves.

Sanjay, without realising it, had stopped all his hobbies like photography and trekking, which he used to really enjoy before he met Tanuja. It wasn't that Tanuja had prevented him from indulging in these activities. But, as newlyweds, they had first been busy setting up a house, after which they had fallen into a pattern of doing things together. Since Tanuja did not particularly enjoy either photography or trekking, without Sanjay realising it, these things had taken a backseat. His weekends now revolved around doing things that she wanted and he had had enough. Perhaps he didn't know how to articulate it better, and stormed out instead.

A Bollywood movie I once saw had a perfect couple who dressed similarly, thought alike and did every single thing together. While newlyweds are usually the ones displaying the joined-at-the-hip phenomenon, there are others in long-term relationships too who think love means never having to be apart.

In the initial stages of a relationship, fuelled by dopamine-crazed feelings of euphoria, this might be the norm rather than the exception, as it had been with Sanjay and Tanuja. But as time goes on, it will become a boxed-in-fenced-in-no-escape scenario if the couple expects that every single need of theirs will be met by their partner.

While most of us can relate to physical space—we all know that feeling of distinct discomfort when a stranger stands too close in a queue—it is the emotional space that a person in a relationship needs that is harder to understand. It is easy to presume that, if somebody loves you, they would want to spend every waking moment of their time with you or thinking about you, to the exclusion of everybody else.

How much space an individual needs in a relationship is very relative. According to psychologists, it stems back to childhood and the kind of relationship a person had with his/her parents. If it was an anxious relationship, filled with rejection and a need to please, then the person can have a problem with space and might turn out to be too clingy and possessive. If the parents were consistently warm and nurturing, the person may not have any problem spending time apart.

Since there are always two parties in a relationship, the need for space may vary, as each would come with their own set of beliefs about how to spend time together and how much togetherness is too much and how much exclusive time one can claim from their partner. The conflicts arise when one partner feels neglected or left out due to the other's need for space. If a partner expresses their need for space, it might feel like rejection or abandonment to the other. The clingy partner becomes clingier and the partner who is trying to get some space resents it, tries harder to break away, or if that isn't possible, lies about that late office meeting when they have actually been at the pub, having a drink with their friends. If secrecy has already crept into a relationship, then it is a danger sign and a warning. If you cannot tell your partner openly about your need to be with other people, without them, then you have an issue that has to be addressed.

Experts agree that no matter how close you are to your partner, it is essential to have some exclusive time for oneself and separate hobbies, as this fosters a sense of independence and infuses freshness in a relationship, which otherwise is in danger of getting submerged in the grip of the routine and the mundane. When partners have their own sets of friends and time for themselves, they feel happier, as a result of which they are able to give more to the relationship.

Expressing the need for space requires not only courage but also tact. One has to assure the other about why this would help make the relationship stronger. Every person in this world, whether in a relationship or not, has a right to grow and a right to do things that are meaningful to them without their partner always being a part of it. Sanjay had not yet learnt how to express it to Tanuja tactfully. What is more, he had not even realised how he had gradually neglected those hobbies which gave him so much joy before he got married. Marriage requires both individuals to make certain adjustments and sometimes, like in Sanjay's case, it is the hobbies that get sidelined as they aren't seen as something very important.

The need for space is a tightrope walk. Too little might make the relationship claustrophobic and too much can weaken the bond. It is a fine balance, easily upset.

The trick is to take one step at a time, have no secrets, never wander too far and come back with double the love when the need for space is met.

LET'S TALK

Constantly talking isn't necessarily communicating.

–Charlie Kaufman

Why the written word is a catalyst for love

As a child, I used to visit my grandfather's ancestral home in Kerala every summer when my school closed for vacation. He had a huge wooden cupboard that was full of books. None of the grandchildren were allowed to go anywhere near it, except for me. My grandfather felt that I was a responsible child, and would be very careful with his collection of books. He could see my love for the written word and by giving me access to his most treasured possession, his books, he kindled my love further. It was in this cupboard that I discovered a letter that he wrote my grandmother. Surreptitiously I read it, fascinated, thrilled and utterly charmed with the magic of his words on paper, feeling like a little thief to be privy to something so personal, yet not guilty enough to stop reading. I replaced it and never told him that I had come across it, forever committing to memory the magic of that moment.

Anyone who has been in love knows that the urge to communicate with the beloved is intense, unstoppable and something beyond one's control. Lovers use any means at their disposal to reach out to each other. There are so many love letters preserved carefully, emotions pouring out through words on paper, expressing sentiments cherished, capturing thoughts which could otherwise be ephemeral. Trapped within the words are myriad emotions, frozen forever. Such is the charm of a love letter.

In ancient times we had carrier pigeons. Anacreon, a Greek poet who lived more than two thousand years ago, spoke of infatuation, love, disappointments and also made everyday observations about people in his poetry. In one of his poems, he describes the flight of the pigeon which drank from his cup, ate from his hand, flew around his home and slept on his lyre. It was this pigeon, so very dear to him, that he used as a messenger to convey his emotions to his beloved, when he fell in love.

The spoken word exists only in memories which may fade with time or with the death of the person, but the written word remains. In India, the earliest love letter on non-perishable material was found in a cave in Ramgarh hills, in Sarguja district in Madhya Pradesh. It is engraved in Brahmi script and dates back to the third century BC. It is a letter from a young sculptor, expressing his feelings to his lady-love, a temple maid or Devdasi.

In Indian mythology, letters have played an important part in uniting lovers. Rukmini, in order to escape an unwanted marriage to Sishupala, writes a love letter to Krishna and sends it through a trusted messenger, Sunanda. In the letter, Rukmini asks Krishna to kidnap her while she is on her way back from the temple, because she does not want unnecessary warfare. Krishna obliges, and the two are united.

As adolescents, most of us have passed on little love notes to the ones we fancy, sometimes directly and sometimes through wingmen, giggling, watching out for 'dangers' in the form of particularly suspicious teachers or, worse, the headmaster. In the present day, these notes have been replaced by text messages, but the essence of what they say remains the same.

When in love, you want to spend every minute of your time with that person, a call from them sends your heart soaring, and separation seems like torture. You yearn to be with them, look at them and simply hear their voice. Napoleon, in one of his letters to Josephine, says: *'Since I left you, I have been constantly depressed. My happiness is to be near you. Incessantly I live over in my memory your caresses, your tears, and your affectionate solicitude.'*

The emotions that today's lovers undergo are no different from the ones that Napoleon did. However, the only difference is that Napoleon, Rukmini and Anacreon had no way of knowing if their beloveds got the messages they sent or not, till the messenger came back and communicated to them that they had, or till they got a reply in return.

Present-day lovers have it a lot easier. Communication is instant. Almost all the IM apps even tell you whether the message has been read or not. If lovers in olden times waited for the flutter of a pigeon's wings or the ring of a postman's cycle to tell them that they had got mail, the present-day couple waits for a ping or a buzz from their phone or the laptop telling them the same, just like Tom Hanks and Meg Ryan in *You've Got Mail*.

While browsing my newsfeed on Facebook, I came across a young man's status message that read, 'Happiness is when "last seen at" changes to "online" and then "typing".' I couldn't resist posting a reply to that. My comment read, 'But true liberation and freedom comes when you no longer feel a need to check out the "last seen at" stamp.'

The only question that remains is whether one really wants to be *that* liberated. After all, love is a potent drug—addictive, exhilarating, all-consuming and mostly unstoppable.

And everyone knows when the phone buzzes, how hard it is to resist checking it.

How nagging affects a relationship

'Darling, will you water the garden?'
'I will.'
'When?'
'In a bit.'
After half an hour:
'Have you watered the garden yet?'
'No. I said I would do it.'
After forty minutes:
'How many times do I have to ask you to water the garden? If you can't do it, just say so.'
'I told you I will do it. Now stop nagging.'

Anyone who has been married for a while would be very familiar with their own personalised version of the above scenario and also with the three magic words, 'Please don't nag.' A popular visual doing the rounds on social media says, 'Ladies, if a man says he will do it, he will. There is no need to remind him every six months.'

It is as though a few months after the couple gets married and the rose-tinted glasses come off, any communication to make the other party do something has to be repeated over and over. Marriage bestows upon you the gift of selective hearing. You hear only that which you want to, filtering the rest out like those high-end Quiet Comfort noise-cancelling headphones. The frustrated spouse who wants to be heard turns up either the frequency of the request or the volume, both of which result in scratchy interruptions to an otherwise smooth-flowing marital melody. Like it or not, when two people are married to each other—or living with each other—that little thing called nagging enters the picture sooner or later and becomes an integrated part of coupledom like the serpent between Adam and Eve in the Garden of Eden.

Indian women had their worst suspicions confirmed when they woke up on the morning of 8 March 2014—International Women's Day—to news of a study conducted by the Organisation for Economic Co-operation and Development, which said that the average Indian man spends just nineteen minutes a day on routine housework (unsurprisingly, among the lowest in the world). The average Indian woman spends a whopping 298 minutes on the same. It conjured up in my mind a cartoon which depicts a hassled, annoyed mother standing in a kitchen, three pots on the stove, a baby on her hip, and a toddler bawling its lungs out at her feet, and her answering the phone saying, 'Can I call you back in five years?'

Another cartoon that did the rounds—not in response to the above—said: 'Men are like fine wine. They start out as grapes and it is up to women to stomp the juice out of them until they turn into something acceptable to have dinner with.'

Juxtapose all the above and it isn't hard to see why women have to stomp men and pulp them into affable companions, never mind even if it is the subdued 'whatever you say, darling' kinds that they frustratingly metamorphose into with incessant nagging, threats and nudges.

The stereotype of the nagging wife has existed for many centuries now. She has lived in folk tales, popular cartoons, jokes, television soaps, movies and literature. She is accompanied by a henpecked man, who is pitied, ridiculed or empathised with, depending on the marital status of the viewer.

Grandmothers and well-meaning aunts advise young brides to 'train their husbands well' to help in household chores and not to let their roving eyes wander. The presumption here is that men are little boys who never grow up and hence need to be nudged, shepherded and guided on daily chores. A few years down the line, the young bride, now no longer young but a whole lot wiser, discovers that there is only so much she can do in terms of controlling her little-boy-man who has a mind of his own. If in the earlier years, her wish was his instant command, she discovers that she must now make repeated requests as he has sunk deep into the plush, luxurious comfort of the conjugal couch and needs a huge helping hand to budge even a tiny bit.

Thus begins the Catch-22 nag-repeat-nag cycle.

Nagging can be the cacophonous, 'Do it right now, how many times do I have to remind you' kind, which makes the man drop the TV remote and jump up to head in the direction of the chore-chart taped on the fridge, or it can be the passive-aggressive, silent kind, where the bewildered man gets a cold 'Nothing' as a reply to his 'What's wrong, darling?'. The former produces instant results and buys peace while the latter lingers in the air, the chore undone till a light bulb goes off in his head, hopefully shining its spotlight on the task that had to be tick-marked three weeks ago.

After a few weeks, if the nagging has shown no effects, the woman either throws up her hands in despair or begins a fight the size of the iceberg that sunk the *Titanic*. If the man is wise, he does not let things get to this state. He would have pacified her early enough by getting off the sofa and putting in his nineteen minutes, thus deftly navigating past the iceberg which would have otherwise caused a catastrophe.

No woman likes to be called a nag. It is a somewhat derogatory term which brings to mind a whiny, complaining, domineering kind of a person, metaphorically holding a rolling pin over an innocent, meek, subdued man who says, 'Yes dear' to a command of, 'Darling, bring me my bathroom slippers'. Interestingly, there exists no such equivalent of a controlling husband. When a man asks something of his wife, it is a request. But if she reminds him of a chore not done—after doing her fair share of laundry, child-minding, cooking and tidying—it is 'nagging'.

Socrates had famously said, 'By all means marry. If you get a good wife, you will become happy. If you get a bad one, you will become a philosopher.' He had no choice but to be a philosopher. But that was probably only because he did not have the option of sly-posting sarcastic cartoons on social media and no studies to tell him that he better get his sleeves rolling and pitch in with the housework.

How anger affects relationships

Holding on to anger is like grasping a hot coal with the intent of throwing it at someone else. You are the one who gets burnt.

—Gautama Buddha

IN THE WHOLE GAMUT of human emotions, anger is one of the most destructive ones. When you first encounter something that makes you angry, a primitive part of your brain, the amygdala, is the first to respond. The amygdala then alerts the body and, much like an action hero, the adrenalin glands get pumped, accelerating the chemical rush, increasing the heart rate and the blood flow to your brain and muscles. The body also releases testosterone and you begin to speak louder and faster, while your facial expression changes into a menacing frown, making you sport an ominous look, sending a warning to those around you. Even if you do manage to control your anger and do not shout but grind your teeth and 'bear it', you are still harbouring resentment and burying it till a trigger sets it off the next time.

According to researchers and evolutionary scientists, we are programmed to pick up clues of anger instantaneously—infants as young as six months can tell the difference between an angry adult face and a happy one. Unhappy or angry faces trigger a response from the right side of the brain and a smiling face triggers a response from the left. In a study conducted in 2009, subjects were shown two androgynous faces with different expressions. One face had lowered eyebrows and pursed lips and the other had a smile. The majority of the subjects identified the angry face as that of a male and the other as that of a female, even though there were no other identifying facial characteristics. Anger is associated with masculinity and the deluge of movies showing the 'angry young male' fuels the idea that somehow anger is acceptable if you are a man. If it is a woman who is displaying anger, it is attributed to 'hormones' or 'that time of the month'.

Anger can be a useful thing at times. For example, if you see someone being harassed and you speak up or try and call the authorities because you are furious, then the action that stems out of anger is something positive. However, when it comes to relationships, most of the time what happens is a knee-jerk reaction, hurting and harming the ones we love. Everybody gets angry once in a way. But if one of the partners is angry frequently, then it is time to take stock and analyse what the triggers are.

The most common cause for anger in relationships is the feeling of entitlement; that one person has the right to tell the other what to do as 'he/she is mine'. Everything that is in agreement with the angry person's thought process is met with approval and anything that is not puts them in a rage.

If there is no power struggle between a couple then they are able to talk about what it is that makes them angry and are able to reach an amicable solution. But if one of the partners is close-minded and rigid in their thinking, refusing to look at the situation from the other person's point of view, then either they fight constantly or they internalise it, burying the issue without really addressing it. Either way, it grows into resentment and frustration over a period of many years, finally eroding the very foundations of a relationship, which is love and trust. Eventually the partners grow distant and the relationship crumbles.

In relationships, a common occurrence is blame. 'I wouldn't be so angry if you would just listen to me'; 'Why can't you at least hear me out?'; 'You know I do not like this and yet you do it' are all phrases that are often heard. People do this as they do not want to take responsibility for their reactions. One can choose not to react in a certain way, whenever your partner does something that annoys you. But the knee-jerk reaction is to attack the other person and peg the blame on them, telling them that if they had behaved in the manner expected, then one would not have got annoyed or irked.

The other common occurrence is generalised statements like, 'You *always* do that'; 'You *always* say this'; 'You *never* do this'. If examined logically, it is likely that what the person is saying is highly exaggerated. Yet they believe it is true at that point as anger has clouded their judgement, which also explains why we blurt out things in anger, which we later regret.

Anger, if not addressed, slowly kills love. If you care about the relationship, it is time to kill the anger. Like Kahlil Gibran said, 'If your heart is a volcano, how shall you expect flowers to bloom?'

Why we talk the way we do

IT WAS DECEMBER, MY favourite time of the year. The weather in Bangalore was a perfect amalgamation of all things happy—cool enough to send a shiver down your spine but not so cold for you to freeze to death if you don't have your warm woollies on. I had an invitation to attend my twenty-fifth year high school reunion and I did not want to pass up the chance to revel in nostalgia. At the reunion, I met many of my classmates after a gap of two decades, and it was a huge slide down memory lane. It left me with goose bumps and a silly smile on my face which refused to go away even three days after the event.

I had another attack of memories as I was cleaning the attic a few days after the reunion. I discovered an old box of letters that my spouse and I had written to each other twenty years ago when we first met. After the children had gone to bed we sat up late like two excited children, reading all that we had written and laughing out loud. There were hundreds of letters, as this was the time before the internet. We were living in different cities at that time and, if we had to communicate, it was through good old snail-mail, hand-written and hand-delivered by the friendly neighbourhood postman.

Back then, we were forced to be patient. And I think that was a good thing. Judging by the number of letters I wrote my husband, I can only imagine what I would have been like had instant messaging existed during my courtship days. I'm sure I would have hounded him, stalked him, bullied him, nagged him, frequently asked why he hadn't replied to a message even though a whole fifteen minutes had passed, and told him not to lie to me as I could see that he was online. The poor guy would have probably run in the opposite direction.

I can tell you a thing or two that I did not know back then: most men do not like to be hounded and to be constantly on call. Women communicate in a way different to men. Several studies have shown this to be true. A woman who is madly in love with a guy might think that she is being very caring if she calls and texts him every hour just to know what he is doing and whether he is okay. But he, for sure, would find this behaviour clingy—and nobody likes a clingy paramour. It is important to give him his space and have yours.

A woman who needs her space will also vouch that this is true. The guy might think that he is being protective and loving if he texts her every half hour, asking her what she is doing and telling her that he is missing her. But she—particularly if she is working on something important—will find it annoying. There is a fine line between sharing because you care so much and being over-communicative. Like Kahlil Gibran said, 'Let there be spaces in your togetherness, and let the winds of the heavens dance between you. Love one another but make not a bond of love. Let it rather be a moving sea between the shores of your souls. Fill each other's cup but drink not from one cup. The oak and the cypress do not grow in each other's shadows.'

According to neuroscientists, men and women's brains are wired differently but that does not make one gender smarter than the other. Men have more synapses connecting the cells in one part of the brain than women do. Research shows that men do better than women in spatial perception but women have a better verbal memory and fluency. Perhaps this would explain why it is so important for a woman to talk to the guy she cares about or is falling in love with. Women tend to be detail-oriented. Thus a guy when asked what he did that morning might just say he went shopping, whereas if you ask a woman the same question, she will probably tell you that she stepped out to buy sparkly glitters, but there was a sale going on for some dresses which her best friend's sister had bought and found to be a great bargain, and so she thought she would try them on, but they did not have it in her size, but she tried on the next size anyway and it fit, and so do you think she has gained weight. And oh yes, she did find the sparkly glitter but she thought she would wait till next week as the shopkeeper—a real nice chap—said that they would go on sale then. If you are nodding your head with familiar understanding of this concept, congratulations, you have a woman in your life who genuinely cares about you.

A well-known piece by Dave Barry talks about a man and a woman who have been dating each other for six months. While driving back from a movie, the woman asks the man whether he realises that they have been seeing each other six months. The man mumbles something and then becomes silent. In his head he thinks that if it has been six months since they started seeing each other, then it means that the car needs an oil change as he last changed it before he started dating her. But the woman misunderstands his silence and wonders if she shouldn't have said anything. She proceeds to beat herself up mentally about how he might think that she meant that she wants more out of the relationship and that she now wants some kind of a commitment. He continues to sit in silence thinking about the automobile bill that he will run up and remembers the large amount that they charged the last time. The woman sees his angry expression and is more and more convinced that her innocuous statement has made him angry. She is on the verge of tears while he, totally unaware of all these thoughts hurtling through her head at the speed of a rocket blasting into space, stares vacantly ahead and continues to drive.

Though the scene above is humorous, it does strike a chord as most of us can relate to it. My guy friends tell me that it is hard to understand women. They find them complicated and also tell me that it is impossible to please a woman. My spouse surprisingly agrees with that one. My women friends tell me with a knowing sigh, 'Aah, he is a man after all. What can you expect? They are like kids and have to be handled that way.' It seems to me that both Mars and Venus have a long way to go to meet on a middle ground.

In *A Cultural Approach to Interpersonal Communications*, Deborah Tannen talks about how a man's expectation from a relationship is different from that of a woman's. She illustrates her point by citing a stock cartoon where a husband and wife are at the breakfast table; the husband is reading the newspaper and the wife is glaring at the back of it, with the husband being blissfully oblivious to her needs and her seeking a bit of his attention. In another Dagwood strip, Blondie complains that he won't even know that she exists and all that matters to him is the newspaper. Dagwood, while reading the paper, reassures her that it is not true and that he loves her. And with those words, he inadvertently pats the paw of the family dog, which his wife has placed there before she left the room. Tannen says a vast majority of people recognise their own experience in them, no matter what culture one is from.

For women, the seeds of friendship are sown when they confide in each other, share information and talk and tell each other what happened that day. Tannen says that when you ask a woman who her best friends are, she is likely to name the women she converses with and confides in on a daily basis. However, when you ask a man the same question, he will usually reply that his best friend is his wife.

Men talk to exchange information. A man believes that communication should have a clear purpose. Every conversation should have a point that is being made. Women talk to bond. They talk to express what they are feeling. For women, talking is a way of expressing closeness.

'When a man says yes, he means yes. When a woman says yes, she might mean a thousand things which you have to decipher based on many factors such as tone, body language, the emphasis and duration of the syllable stressed while pronouncing the word,' quipped my best friend who I also happen to be married to. I laughed as I knew he had a point even though I did not admit it to him.

Years ago, I used to work with children and I noticed a distinct difference in the games that little boys and little girls played. I wondered what made them choose those particular games. Sheila Steinberg, in *An Introduction to Communication Studies*, stresses that the seeds of behaviour in adult life are sown in childhood. Most little girls prefer games like 'house' and 'school' and 'hospital', where the emphasis is on a few rules and a lot of communication. There are no losers or winners and everyone gets a turn. Thus in a game like 'classroom', one of the girls is the teacher and even the most shy one in the group gets included as one of the students; or in a game like 'house-house' where they pretend to be adults who have their own kids and they visit each other. You cannot win or lose at these games as they are non-competitive. Boys, on the other hand, prefer games like soccer, cricket and basketball where there are clear rules, clear losers and winners and very little talk is needed.

However, it has to be stated that not all men are competitive and not all women are sensitive and uncompetitive. The differences described are not absolute. But if we bear in mind that men and women do communicate differently, chances of understanding what that long-drawn 'yes' means when it comes from a woman is greater than when you are groping in the dark without a clue.

Women love to talk, you see. But not just to anybody. Only to the guys they care about.

Coming back to that box in the attic, I think I now know why I felt compelled to keep sending my husband letters. I just had to tell him every detail of my life. I must have sent him more than two hundred letters. I must add that he wrote back too. Only that his responses were sometimes store-bought cards.

Why laughter is important in a relationship

FOR A RELATIONSHIP TO sustain itself, one thing that is just as important as love is laughter. Laughter makes it fun. Laughter is the shortest distance between two hearts and laughter is a gift that you find in the most unexpected places. It surprises you like an unexpected shower on a hot summer afternoon. And before you realise it, it is gone leaving you with sweet memories that sometimes last a lifetime. Laughter is something I seek out consciously and strangely I have discovered that when you seek it, you do find it. Okay, I confess—if I don't find it, I orchestrate things to make it happen. *Tee-hee. Ha-ha!*

The women in my family have an innate ability to laugh at just about anything. I remember how much my grandmother used to laugh. You only had to tell her something remotely funny and she would chuckle and guffaw and soon we would all join in. Laughter, like yawning, is infectious.

My mother too has inherited this trait and she has a terrific sense of humour, often childlike, extremely funny, and you clutch your sides laughing at something she said or something she did.

When we were children, one of her favourite activities was to startle one of us with a loud bang, made by bursting a brown paper bag or a plastic cover. She would fill it with air and twist the ends so that it looked like a balloon. And then when we were least expecting it, she would creep up quietly behind us and burst it.

My brother and I learnt quickly to anticipate it. It would usually be on a day we had bought pure peaberry coffee powder (without chicory); it came in a brown bag which was an ideal size for filling with air and bursting. The temptation was irresistible for her. When we became smarter and learnt to avoid her little bang-expedition, she found a new victim—my dad. No matter how many times she did it, my poor father would be caught unaware. He would be reading the newspaper intently or would be studying a magazine with stock-market data and my mom would creep up behind him, with my brother and me suppressing our giggles in the background. She would then burst the paper bag. BANG! The explosion would be deafening and Dad would be so startled he would drop the paper or magazine. When he had recovered, he would join in the delighted, mad and absolutely crazy laughter. He was always a sport.

My children soon learnt what a fun activity it actually was. Many years back, my son came back from school with a sheepish look saying he had been punished in class but he enjoyed it so much that he wouldn't mind getting punished again for doing it. When asked what he had done, he said he had—yes, you guessed it—burst a paper bag in the middle of math class, nearly sending the teacher rocketing into space, he added gleefully. I suppressed my urge to laugh and told him sternly that he should respect the teacher and never repeat it again. With that I dusted my hands of parenting duty and as soon as he was out of earshot, I called up my mother, narrated it to her and we both burst into delighted chuckles.

I don't burst paper covers like my mom (okay, I admit, I have done it a couple of times, but *only* a couple), but one thing that I love to do is hide behind doors when someone is entering the room and then shout 'BOOOO' and jump out suddenly. I am sure many of you must have done it too at some point in your lives. It is hilarious to see the look of surprise on the face of the person and then watch it change to shocked relief. Usually the person joins in the laughter. I have startled my friends and cousins many times like this and then gone into paroxysms of laughter at this very childish prank.

Once when I saw my husband's car pulling up in the driveway, on an impulse I decided that it was the perfect opportunity to play this trick on him especially as he has an unvarying routine of never ringing the doorbell, but instead letting himself in with his key. Then he enters the house and calls out for me.

That day when I saw his car pulling up, I swiftly hid behind the door so that the moment he put his key in, opened the door and entered, I could pounce out—like a panther, I thought wickedly—and shout 'Grrrrr' or

'Bowwww' or 'Booooo' or whatever noise struck me as most appropriate at that point. I imagined striking terror in his heart with my decibel level and, heart racing, I positioned myself, listening carefully for his footsteps and the click of the key in the door. The moment he stepped in, with perfect timing I jumped out like a Jack in the Box and let out an ear-shattering 'BHHHHHOOOOOOW'. The person who jumped into the air wasn't my husband (he was used to my crazy ways after all) but a very startled insurance salesman who had accompanied my husband home so they could go over, in detail, a policy my husband was interested in.

He must have got the fright of his life, poor guy, at this crazy woman who his potential client was married to, and I think it was only his eagerness to sell the policy that prevented him from throwing his hands up in the air and running out screaming in terror. My husband was trying his best to suppress his laughter and I really could not control it. I ran into the kitchen, out of their sight, and collapsed laughing on the floor.

Like I was telling you, laughter springs up on you when you least expect it, or maybe it is because I orchestrate it with precise (okay, sometimes impulsive) planning.

But hey—what's life (and relationships) without laughter?

Why respect is important in a relationship

JEENA AND KISHORE HAVE been together for fifteen years, eleven of which they have been married. They have two children, an eight-year-old, and a six-year-old. Of late their marriage has run into troubled waters. They are not able to connect to each other the way they once did.

'When we do speak to each other, it seems to be a huge effort and we tend to end up fighting,' confessed Jeena.

I was surprised. I had always thought of them as a couple that was so much in sync with each other's needs and often admired the way they communicated.

'Maybe it is just a phase,' I consoled, not knowing what to say.

'No ... it is just that I feel so disrespected in this relationship. It is like he has presumed so many things about me. Anything that I say is never taken seriously. He just laughs it off like it is a big joke.'

'Was it always like this or did it change slowly?' I asked.

'In the beginning I did not mind it much. I just thought it was his way of lightening the situation. Later the children came along and we were busy raising them. So I don't think I really noticed. But now that the children are fairly independent and do not need me so much, I find that our communication styles have changed. I don't know when it changed into something so unbearable for me,' she said.

Her words stayed with me and I remembered her at the Bangalore Literature Festival, where I was one of the panellists in a session that included a psychiatrist and a relationship counsellor and two eminent women writers, both of whom write novels that deal with love and relationships. At the end of a very entertaining and meaningful discussion, the floor was thrown open to the audience for questions. A lady asked, 'How do you define respect in a relationship? How important is it?'

I answered her question at that point, as did the psychiatrist who said that it was one of the key-stones of a relationship, without which it would crumble. Our replies satisfied her but later I mulled about it more.

There are boundaries in any relationship. These boundaries, even in the most intimate relationships, have to be honoured, or else bitterness is bound to creep in. In a romantic relationship, respect essentially means recognising and honouring the boundaries that your partner has set—whether it comes to physical boundaries, verbal exchanges or behaving in a certain manner. Your partner needs to feel valued and respected. Over time, without even our realising it, patterns in communication are set and become a habit, and finally resentment creeps in.

For instance, if a woman has repeatedly told the man whom she is in a relationship with that she doesn't like it when he playfully pats her on the derriere and yet he continues to do it, then she is likely to feel disrespected. Here, the action itself is not what may be a big deal, but the fact that her repeated requests are being ignored. Needless to say, if they are not in a relationship, it would straight away be construed as sexual harassment, with the guy being dragged to the higher authorities and appropriate action against him being taken. We tend to tolerate a lot of things we do not like when it comes to the ones we love.

Similarly if a woman persistently corrects her partner's table manners in public, he is sure to feel disrespected. This might seem a tiny thing to crib about in a relationship—after all, she is only correcting it for 'his own good'—but the fact that she is doing it without tact smacks of disrespect. Respect is consideration for your partner's feelings, where you act in a manner so as to not hurt them.

In the 2012 movie *English Vinglish*, directed by Gauri Shinde, the wife (played by Sridevi) makes really tasty laddoos and the husband (played by Adil Hussain) jokingly remarks to a group of guests that his wife was born to make laddoos. Though it hurts her, she does not say anything as he would claim that he was only praising her. But the hurt in her eyes is evident as she silently carries the platter inside. She feels disrespected but is unable to articulate it. Clearly, a subtle boundary has been crossed.

A conflict is likely to arise if the partners differ in their opinion of the boundaries that they have set. Hence it is important to define boundaries. Since a relationship is at all times a work-in-progress and never a completed masterpiece, it is essential to keep moving these boundaries if the relationship has to evolve to the next level.

One partner may feel that it is perfectly fine to share passwords to email accounts and may feel insulted if the other partner refuses to do so. Similarly, when it comes to mobile phones, one partner may feel it is a violation of their privacy if the other partner reads their messages. But if their partner is the kind who believes in the philosophy of 'what is yours is ours and what is mine is ours', then this would lead to big fights and perhaps even accusations of the other trying to be secretive, for if there is nothing to hide, why shouldn't the passwords be shared?

Dr John Gottman, a leading researcher in marriage and couple issues, says that for a relationship to be healthy, the ratio of positives to negatives should be 5:1. He defines positives as expressions of joy, humour, affection and interest. The negatives are expressions of anger, contempt, whining, sadness or unhappiness with something. Gottman calls this ratio the 'magic ratio'. He says that for every negative feeling or negative interaction between the partners, there must be five positive interactions. Partners who constantly criticise each other or who keep focusing on the negative traits are definitely in a relationship that is unbalanced. Gottman suggests that in order to increase the positives, the couple should make a conscious effort. For example, if a partner comes home after a long day and wants to talk about what happened, the other one should pay attention and ask questions and really listen, instead of nodding absently from in front of the television. He suggests keeping a journal to record positive and negative interactions, and reviewing it at the end of the week. Quantifying the interactions and assessing them mathematically will give a clear picture and the couple can then make amends.

But this doesn't mean that one should not criticise or express dissatisfaction. However, one has to do it with respect towards one's partner. And one has to balance it out by appreciating all that is going right. Communication is vital to a relationship. Trusting that your partner has good judgement, has your best interests at heart, and wanting the best for your partner should come above all else if the relationship is to last.

So should treating your partner with utmost respect at all times—even when you think that they sometimes do not deserve it.

How expectations twist a relationship

Five of my friends have been through a divorce, their marriages lasting from a couple of years to more than a decade. While two have remarried and now have children with their current partners, three are single and haven't decided whether or not they will marry again. When newlyweds post 'happy couple' pictures on social media sites, I always think there is an invisible caption which nobody notices that reads: *'Happy for now. May not be so tomorrow.'* It might be a cynical view to take—after all, when a couple gets married they do believe with all their heart that it is going to last forever and nothing, just nothing can come between their love. They feel elated and lucky to have found 'The One' and, in their eyes, their partner is perfect. That's why weddings are such joyous occasions, with happy families and happier friends joining in the celebrations; there is much revelry, bonhomie and a general feeling of hope, love and laughter.

In the 2005 romantic comedy movie *Wedding Crashers,* it is precisely this feeling that two friends, Jeremy (Vince Vaughn) and John (Owen Wilson), who are divorce mediators, take advantage of when they gatecrash weddings to drink for free and to scout for women to sleep with. Their plan hits a bump when they themselves get into relationships.

Relationships are a lot of hard work. The couple doesn't live in a cocoon. After the initial honeymoon phase ends, most land on Earth with a gentle thud. Except that sometimes the thud isn't gentle at all, but an alarming wake-up call. Buried deep not only in love but also in each other's eyes, the pair now discovers the practical side of living together.

Take for instance the finances. If both partners are earning, how should the money issues be sorted? Should there be joint accounts? Or should it be individual accounts with an arrangement for one to take care of the rent, and the other to pay the grocery bills? Or maybe a common kitty into which each deposits a certain amount? What if you have fundamental ideological differences with your partner? What if you are a grasshopper who believes in living life to the fullest, spending lavishly on travel, luxuries and everything that gives you joy, while your partner is the kind that believes in making large nest eggs for rainy days which may never occur? Numerous studies have shown that money is a major cause of disagreement between couples.

It gets even more complicated if the couple decides to have children and, when the children arrive, the issues that arise are not merely confined to finances alone. If it were so, relationships would be such a cakewalk! There are decisions to be taken right from whether to use diapers or not, whether to go with commercially-available baby-food or the traditional fare that grandmothers made, whether to hire a nanny or look after the child yourself, and many such. As the children grow up, the really important decisions, of choosing pre-schools or at a later date, schools and colleges, enter the picture.

In the early years, the children listen to their parents. As they grow up, they begin to develop their own personalities with their individual likes and dislikes. You expect them to behave in a certain manner—after all, it is you who raised them—but they may not agree with you. The couple should jointly decide on the rules, the acceptable norms of behaviour, manners, the expectations in terms of academics and pocket money—if it ought to be given at all, and if it should, how much and whether one needs to monitor what it is being spent on. Stephen Covey, in his bestseller *The 7 Habits of Highly Effective Families,* talks about making effective choices that will create higher thoughts and a wider perspective. He talks about increasing the space between what happens to you and your response to it, in order to have more meaningful interactions with the ones you love.

All of this has to be balanced with the couple's individual careers, travel plans, promotions, pay-rises, targets and other commitments—a huge cause of stress by itself—apart from domestic arrangements which usually involve a cook, a driver and a maid if you happen to be living in a country like India where labour is affordable.

The balance is a precarious one and family life often makes one feel like a juggler walking the tightrope, trying not to lose one's balance or drop any balls. But the fact remains that despite all the juggling and balancing required, for most people, a family is one of life's greatest blessings. Barbara Bush, in her book *Reflections: Life After the White House,* says, 'At the end of your life you will never regret not having passed one more test, not winning one more verdict, or not closing one more deal. You will regret time not spent with a husband, a friend, a child or a parent.'

If there exists a formula to get it perfectly right, it can be safely stated that it is yet to be discovered. The burden of expectations is carried by all who are in relationships. We expect things to run smoothly. We expect others to behave the way we want them to, more so if they happen to be your partner or your family. We expect their choices to resonate with ours. The dissonance when this fails to happen is directly proportional to the weight of the burden that you carry. Heavier the burden, greater the disappointment.

The trick is to enjoy the tightrope walk, being there for each other, never losing sight of the finish line (which is 'till death do us part'), and keeping a large safety net to catch that ball in case it ever drops.

Why it is important to express what you feel

Rashmi and Tarun are both single; they work in the same organisation and spend a lot of time together on common projects. They always eat lunch together, as part of a group, and it is obvious to everyone but themselves that they are drawn to each other. Both refuse to declare their feelings, claiming they are nothing more than colleagues. Deep down, Rashmi wants to take the first step and ask Tarun out for a movie date. But she is so afraid of what he will say that she would rather suffer in silence than ask him outright. She drops big hints, telling him that there is a movie she is dying to see and it is playing that weekend, but so far he hasn't picked up on her hints.

'But what is the worst that can happen if you ask him?' I ask her.

'He might just think I am a lunatic and then I would appear like a fool. After that, imagine the embarrassment of working with him on the same projects,' she replies.

'But he might be equally interested in you and it might be the start of a great relationship,' I point out.

'Or we might find that we have nothing to talk about other than projects,' she sighs.

In a novel that I recently read, a single woman becomes pregnant accidentally and decides to take a holiday. She stays in a beautiful cottage in Suffolk and eventually strikes up a friendship with her neighbour, who is struggling to cope with her husband's irritability, bad temper and mood swings as he has had an accident and is upset about no longer being the breadwinner of the family. Another woman from the same village has lost her mother as well as her boyfriend and has moved back home to sell her mother's cottage and soothe her ailing heart. She is crazily attracted to a guy in the village who is single and available but she doesn't have the courage to confess what she feels. The pregnant woman is afraid to pick up the phone and call the father of her baby. She is even terrified of sending him an email. So she finally gathers her courage and writes him a letter and then debates whether or not to drop it in the mailbox.

What struck me was that all these women had one thing in common: they were scared to act aggressively, afraid to express without mincing words all that was going on inside their heads, fearing consequences that would not be in their favour. So they chose to wait and let things take their own course. Though the above story is fictional, it draws from real life and most of us have experienced that little moment of self-doubt where we keep mum, even though we want to speak up because we are afraid that our actions or words might be misconstrued by the other party.

Why it is important to express what you feel

Very often, in a relationship, we presume that the other person knows our needs and will act in the manner that we desire. This rarely happens. Experts say that the most common reason for miscommunication in a relationship is that we fail to realise how little we have actually communicated. Psychologists have a term for this. They call it 'signal amplification bias'. Several studies have been conducted which have demonstrated that when people fear rejection, they tend to perceive that they have communicated much more romantic interest than they actually have to a potential partner.

Thus the chap who is asking a woman he is drawn to what her plans are for the weekend instead of telling her that he would love to catch a movie with her and when would she be free is cushioning his chances of rejection. If she replies that she is free, it might prompt him to ask her out for a movie. But if she says that she is going shopping, it gives him a chance to say that he is planning to watch a game with his friends.

Even in the best of relationships, there is always a chance of being misunderstood. Research shows that a staggering 55 per cent of our communication happens non-verbally—our facial expression, gestures, eye-contact, posture and tone of voice. When we interact with others, we are saying a lot even when we do not speak. When there is a chance of miscommunication even when we are face to face with somebody, which is the best of circumstances, imagine the scope for miscommunication to occur when you are connecting through other mediums like IM, emails and chats, where there are no visual clues apart from emoticons and cute stickers with puppies, penguins, octopuses and other cartoon characters screaming things like 'Epic' and 'You are awesome'. An extra exclamation mark, a misplaced comma or forgetting to type a smiley at the end of what you think is a witty remark could all go into the cauldron of things-gone-wrong.

While non-verbal communication happens naturally, whether we think about it or not, what we say—or type, as the case may be—does make a difference. We need to choose our words carefully. We also need to choose those emoticons well.

After all, what we say and, more importantly, what we do not say has the power to change our worlds forever.

And sometimes reading between the lines and diving straight in makes all the difference.

How often should you message a person you fancy?

ANJALI, TWENTY-NINE, WAS IN the very early stages of something that could blossom into a relationship. It was a guy she'd met at a party and he was insanely attracted to her. I, being her friend and being the older, more experienced one, was promptly appointed her official advisor on all matters of the heart and it became my duty to guide her on her replies to his messages. Bubbling with joy and excitement, she would read out every single text he sent and we would discuss it and what her response should be in detail.

I would stop her from sending more than two messages unless he had replied. 'You know the rule. Treat them mean, keep them keen,' I said.

'What nonsense, I am dying to text him. I so want to.'

'Why did you appoint me your advisor then? If you don't listen to me, I shall quit. You handle this on your own,' I threatened.

'No, appointed advisors aren't allowed to quit.'

'Then you have to listen to your appointed advisor. I write on these things and, trust me, I know how this stuff works. You will thank me later.'

Reluctantly she would oblige. And sure enough, whatever I predicted the guy would do happened, and we would both giggle like teenagers, plotting and planning her next move.

Fortunately for me, Anjali got what she wanted and they are now in a relationship. I have no idea whether my navigation of their initial exchanges helped or not but I claimed credit for it. The relationship game is indeed one of strategy and smart moves—at least in the early stages.

If you have ever been in a relationship, you would know the rule in that beginning stage—you message only if they do. If they write a ten-word message, you make sure you reply with not more than fifteen words at the most. If they do not message you back, you do not send a third, fourth and a fifth. (A second might still be worth a try—perhaps they are genuinely busy.) We all know that wait-by-the-phone stage in a relationship, where you long for their message, call, text or any manner of reaching out, as long as they do reach out to you. And when the reply finally comes, you are beside yourself with joy and, mentally stumbling over thoughts that gush like water from a tap that has been dry for long, you text back with gusto, your heart doing a flip, leaping high in the air.

The other day an invite for a book launch landed in my inbox. It was a fairly high-profile one—the author being somebody with great connections and an impressive who's who guest list—with all the frills and fancies that accompany an event like that. I would have loved to attend except that the launch was happening in Mumbai, which is seven hundred miles from where I live and, no, flight tickets weren't included as part of the invite. Barely had I turned back to write, when another invite for the same event landed up in my inbox. Then another. And yet another. All the invites were identical! Finally I was forced to bring it to the notice of the sender that my inbox was being inundated with the same invite to an event I couldn't attend due to constraints of time and that little thing called finance-management, the basic tenet of which is to prioritise your spending.

The sender was apologetic. She did not know that the invite was quietly doing a replica of Ravan's heads and multiplying in a geometric series while she was busy sending them out to other people. It reminded me of the desperateness of people in love and to what extents they go to reach out to the other.

In this technology-saturated era, you do not have to just hang around waiting for someone to message you back after the text you sent them. We live in an age of choices. You can lust for them on Tinder, pine for them on OKCupid, admire their intelligence on Twitter, stalk them on Facebook and send a few 'awwws' their way on Pinterest. If all else fails, you can add them to your circles on Google + , and inhale the very online internet air that they do, consoling yourself that it isn't over yet—just that they are yet to notice you exist.

When they finally do pay some attention to you— or your Twitter handle—you have multiple options of wooing too. From sending them a virtual bouquet of flowers or a personalised, tailor-made blanket with their own photos, which you stole from their Facebook profile, to emailing them virtual coupons for a spa in their neighbourhood, the choices are endless. The presumption here is that you wait a little, get to know them a little better and go on a date or two before launching into full-fledged gifting mode.

Sometimes, after a few dates, the conversation and the interest both dry up. The pursuit becomes one-sided. If the person does not get back to you within an anticipated timeframe, then you go all panicky, wondering if they have lost interest. You forget the basic rule and send a second one and, in some desperate cases, a third, fourth and a fifth, through different earlier-mentioned virtual options, much like the invites I got. This is exactly what I had prevented my friend from doing and it paid off. If someone has not replied to you within a couple of hours, it could be because they are genuinely busy. They might be with other people and may not have had a chance to respond. Do not bombard them with an avalanche of messages. That is sure to scare them off. As impatient as you are for a reply, it is best to wait. Do anything but ask them 'why haven't you replied'. They will, eventually, if they are interested enough.

If the replies still don't come, it would be wise to give up and put it behind you, and move on with a bruised ego recycled and salvaged. It will still be functional but not as good as new.

Until the next suitable one comes along and the cycle starts all over again.

How to communicate when there is a conflict

Santosh and Ananya have been living together for two-and-a-half years now. Their folks do not know though. Santosh hails from a small south Indian town and, after he got through CAT, he went to one of the premier management institutes where he met Ananya. She hails from an upper middle class south Indian family. Both intend to tell their parents about the relationship soon and then tie the knot.

We were all chatting the other day and Santosh jokingly remarked that when a woman says 'Nothing is wrong', you could be certain something definitely was. Now how serious it was would depend on other cues like whether she slammed the door, her nostrils were flaring or whether she was quietly humming. Ananya laughed and playfully punched him. I told him that he was sounding like a married man already.

Real life is very different from a fairy-tale romance. Most romantic movies end with the guy getting the girl (or vice versa) and the inference that they live happily ever after. In real life, however, this is where the story begins. The happily-ever-afters are peppered liberally with hard-hitting realities and adjustments to get a relationship from an 'up-in-the-air' zone to a more grounded 'love-actually' one. Each partner carries their baggage of the past and, perching atop it, hopes the differences will decompose like organic waste with love and passion being the super catalysts, so there is a resultant bloom of beautiful red roses or a burst of happy pink magnolias, depending on what you have sown.

The thing about long-term relationships is that they need a lot of hard work, commitment and turning a blind eye to many irritating things which have so much glare that they blind you to a point where even oversized sunglasses with ultra-violet protection does not help. There is no escape as you have committed to the I-do and so you do whatever it takes to keep the wheels rolling smooth, trying to silence the squeaks with generous portions of gritted teeth and understanding, in equal measures.

So, what does it take to keep a relationship going smoothly? Is love alone enough?

According to Terri Orbuch, a clinical psychologist who is also the author of *5 Simple Steps to Take Your Marriage from Good to Great,* there are many myths about relationships, and if you allow yourself to buy into these myths then you rob yourself of happiness in a relationship. One of the biggest myths, according to her, is that your partner should know what you want without your having to articulate it, because he or she loves you. This rarely happens, even with couples who have been together for a long time.

How to communicate when there is a conflict

Once, Santosh made a fried egg for Ananya and she got annoyed with him as she likes the yolk to be fully cooked, and he had made it sunny side up.

'How many times do I have to tell you Santosh—I can't eat this,' she exploded.

'Look, at least I made it for you,' Santosh replied.

Ananya felt that Santosh should have remembered that she hated uncooked egg yolk. Santosh didn't think it was a big deal that he'd forgotten.

In order to communicate better when there are differences of opinion, here are five things that will help:

1. Find fault with the issue, not the person

If you are upset about something and your partner has irked you, the first thing to remember is to focus on the issue, not the person. Thus Ananya could have told Santosh, 'It's nice of you to make this, baby, but would you mind eating it? Or would you mind if I binned it? The half-cooked yolk makes me want to throw up.' Here Ananya has focused on the issue at hand. This is likely to elicit an apology from Santosh and he will perhaps tell her that he will make her another one or would remember the next time. The moment Santosh hears, *'How many times do I have to tell you',* he feels attacked and defensive, and therefore his response.

2. Do not use 'You never…'

Your partner might have done the same thing many times before. Take the very common example of leaving wet towels on the floor. In every relationship, there is sure to be one partner who is tidy and puts away things and the other who cannot be bothered about such finicky details. Instead of beginning the sentence with 'You never...' what you could do is state what you want, without the blame. One could say, 'I feel so good when things are put away and I am in a great mood when the room is tidy. Would you like me to clear up?' At this point, the partner who has made the mess would most probably clear it up. If they don't do it, one has to let go at times and pick up after them. It is very hard to change another person's core habits. This does not mean that one has to pick up after them always. Chances are the other person too is conscious of it and may have genuinely forgotten. If they remember it most of the time, one has to accept it.

3. Be truthful instead of dodging

Sometimes a couple bottles up an issue that is bothering them as they are afraid of upsetting things. Most of us hate conflict and we go to great lengths to avoid them. Acting as if the issue doesn't exist won't work though. Over a period of time it leads to built-up resentment. If something irks you, it is important to express it in a timely manner without blame.

4. Press the pause button

If you are in the middle of a conflict and find yourself getting angrier and angrier, it is best to take a deep breath and leave the room. This way you will avoid blurting out hateful, spiteful things that you don't even mean and which are simply spewed forth in anger. It is important to press the pause button and take a breather. Make it a rule to talk only when calm. When anger enters the picture, make an exit from the scene.

5. Listen

Another thing that happens in conflicts is that one tends not to really listen to what the other person is saying. You are busy making your own point. If your partner is telling you something, rephrase it in your own words and repeat it back to them, saying, 'What I understand is... Am I correct?' This makes them feel heard. If you do not agree with their viewpoint, you could say, 'It is interesting you say that. Could you explain to me why you think so?' This forces them to think and give explanations. Listening helps to put us in the other person's shoes and to see things from their point of view.

Conflicts and miscommunication are bound to crop up in every relationship. It is the ability to handle them and turn them into things that bring you closer and deepen your bond which will take your relationship to that next level.

THREE TO TANGO

Everyone should cultivate a secret garden.

–Esther Perel

How extramarital affairs start

SANDEEP AND SHREYA NEVER meant to get involved with each other. Sandeep has been married twelve years; he has two children, a beautiful wife, a gorgeous home and a soaring career. Shreya is a divorcee with a child and the last thing she wants to do is break up Sandeep's home or be the 'other woman', as her own marriage broke up because of an extramarital affair. Yet they are drawn to each other. Shreya has tried to stay away from Sandeep, as has he. He is riddled with guilt and he cannot understand what it is in Shreya that binds him so, especially when he has a superb relationship with his wife. There really is no cause for him to feel the way he does. He wonders if it is the lure of the forbidden—after all, his marriage is twelve years old. He battles with his feelings and he hopes he is strong enough to not go to bed with Shreya and jeopardise everything that he has. Shreya, on her part, finds that she laughs a lot when she is with Sandeep. He makes her feel ten years younger. It has been a long while since she has found that kind of a connection with anyone. They discuss a lot of things that they have in common, like their love for books and photography. Shreya feels that had they met under different circumstances, Sandeep would have been her ideal man. She is careful to not cross boundaries with him and keeps emphasising that she seeks nothing but his friendship. But in secret she wonders if she is lying to herself.

Time and again we hear of people speaking of deep connections that they form with other people and it usually starts with a stolen glance, a brief chat and a tiny little exchange which they never thought would develop into something this spectacular. Every single connection in this world, other than those that you are born into, starts as a spark is lit. Where it proceeds from then on—whether it grows into a raging fire or whether it smoulders slowly like embers waiting to be fanned—depends on both parties in the relationship.

Social scientists agree that the more time you spend with another person, the more interests you share and conversation you exchange, higher are the chances of falling in love. Thus it is not uncommon to find office romances blossoming under tight deadlines and shared goals. Even if one of the parties to this is in a committed relationship, it is trouble. Unless a conscious decision is taken to keep it to work-related issues alone, it can and often does develop into a full-blown affair. An out-of-town trip, a drink or two more than what one is used to, and a moment of weakness are all it takes for colleagues to turn into lovers. This is the case with extramarital affairs that start outside the work space as well. Often, the couples involved are people who have been neglecting their primary relationship, which becomes mundane when you have been living with the same person for a few years.

In a movie called *What If,* which I loved, Wallace, a medical school dropout (played by Daniel Radcliffe), meets an illustrator called Chantry (Zoe Kazan) and she gives him her phone number as they hit it off well and find each other extremely interesting. Later he walks her home and while saying bye to him, she mentions that her boyfriend will probably be worried as she is late. After he gets home, Wallace sits on his roof, gazing at the stars and lets the paper that has her phone number float away. He is clear that he doesn't want to get involved with anyone who is already in a committed relationship. She meets him again and wants to know why they can't just be friends, and asks him whether her being in a relationship or not negates her qualities as an individual. Isn't she worth more than her relationship status? That poignant exchange left me pondering.

When one is in a committed relationship, there will be numerous chances where you meet people who are interesting. You might share the same interests, have fabulous conversations and genuinely enjoy each other's company. You might be great friends and both of you might be very clear that it is only friendship and nothing more. However, as in the movie and as in the case of Sandeep and Shreya, relationships have a way of developing ever so slowly and creeping into the equation without either of the parties even being aware. Before they realise it, they are in love with each other, and life which was rolling along smoothly till now meets with turbulence and is thrown a little off track. Sandeep and Shreya are still in touch with each other and both know it is only a matter of time before they take it further and end up having sex. The connect they feel with each other is too strong to ignore. They find it impossible to stay away from each other for too long.

If your equation with your current partner is already fragile, a development like this only acts as a catalyst to sever ties and make a fresh start. But if the connection with the partner is strong, then one will acknowledge and admit that things need to be addressed. Maybe staleness has crept into the relationship and this is a warning bell to let in some fresh air. It can come as a wake-up call to both partners to do something about their relationship. If they listen to it and fix their issues, then they are in for a ride which is more secure than before.

However, if they decide to ignore the warning signs, they become yet another statistic in relationships that did not survive.

True love is that which stands the test of time—and of other people invading your space, and how much you permit them to.

How to maintain balance in a relationship

WHILE BIRTHDAY SHOPPING FOR the spouse, I was pleased after a long hunt to finally find something I thought was perfect. The gift-wrapping counter was manned by a girl who was having a rather hard time trying to help out all the customers there as quickly as she could. When my turn finally came, I placed my stuff on the counter and, just as she began wrapping them, a lady cut in and said she needed ten gift vouchers of rupees five thousand each. The girl said the vouchers came only in denominations of five hundred and a thousand, whereupon the lady said that she would take fifty of the thousand-rupee gift vouchers.

    The girl, unable to handle such a request, said that she would have to speak to her superior and dialled for help, while the lady drummed her fingers on the desk and sighed, exclaiming that it wasn't a small amount that she wanted and did the girl realise how late she was getting. I was in a rather benevolent mood and told the girl that I was in no hurry and would wait. The girl smiled and said that at least somebody understood. Then, to my surprise, she proceeded to calmly wrap my gifts, ignoring the lady completely, who fretted, fumed and kept shuffling her feet and sighing in exasperation. The girl shrugged and told her politely that someone else would attend to her shortly.

This little interaction left me thinking as to how similar it is to the choices we make in our behaviour patterns when it comes to relationships. We want to interact with those who are nice to us. We tend to avoid confrontation, doing anything to keep it at bay. Nobody likes a prickly poky porcupine. We gravitate naturally towards those that make us feel loved and wanted.

When two people are in a relationship, they might initially give in to the unreasonable demands of their partners to avoid confrontation, to buy peace. But if one partner inadvertently keeps making demands and the other partner is left always doing the placating, there will come a time when the proverbial last straw will break the camel's back. If the partner is non-confrontational by nature, much like the gift-wrapping girl, they shrug and turn to someone else who can fulfil their needs better. Thus are sown the seeds of an extramarital affair. They find someone who is attentive to them, appreciates them and finds them funny and interesting.

Studies show that most people who are in an extramarital affair never intended to get so involved with someone and never thought they would be that person who cheats on their spouse. They either continue the affair, shrouded in secrecy, feeling giddy with excitement and revelling in it, till it comes to a natural conclusion—where sometimes they move away and sometimes they are discovered. If discovered, then a massive showdown happens. There are bitter words and explosion. Whether the couple survives this or not depends on how strong their relationship is and how much each is willing to make an effort to save it.

A study published in the *Journal of Social and Clinical Psychology* found that, during conflict, couples experience two kinds of concerns. One is a perceived threat and the other is perceived neglect. If a partner is too demanding and critical, the other sees it as a perceived threat. When the partner who feels so moves away—more in a bid to protect themselves from the hurt than to be mean or spiteful—the other sees it as being disloyal, inattentive and not giving enough time to the relationship. The vicious circle thus continues.

The study also found that, in order to make amends, what most people in a relationship wanted was not apologies but to see real intent of wanting to make a change by relinquishing some of the 'power balance'. Thus if a wife feels controlled, her husband buying her flowers may not really work. What she wants is for him to give up or at least try to change that specific behaviour which causes her to feel that way. A husband who feels that the wife nags him a lot wants her to appreciate him a little more for all the things that he does right, rather than pointing out what he gets wrong.

The girl at the gift-wrapping counter felt understood. In a relationship, that is what everyone is looking for: a space to feel secure, understood and loved, and not judged for something beyond one's control. We want to be appreciated for who we are and we all need encouragement from time to time. And when the chips are down, we also need someone to hold us and tell us, 'Hey, hang in there. Things are going to be just fine.'

If there is willingness to compromise, an acceptance of limitations and a genuine intent to understand what the other truly wants, then love multiplies, grows and blossoms slowly like a cherry tree in bloom.

If, on the other hand, the blame game takes over, there is no respite and it collapses faster than a pack of cards. In the dance of relationships, one has to know when to tango, when to foxtrot and when to simply watch from the sides, even as the music plays on.

Can finger length predict a propensity to cheat?

A FEW DAYS BACK Sumana called me up frantic, because her husband's ring finger was longer than his index finger. And that morning's newspaper had published the findings of a study which said that people who have ring fingers longer than their index fingers were more likely to be promiscuous.

According to the team of scientists from Oxford and Northumbria University who led the study, the length of the index finger depends on the level of testosterone—the hormone related to the sex drive—that one has been exposed to in the womb. If the ring finger is longer than the index finger, it is likely that the person had been exposed to more testosterone and hence would have a greater propensity to cheat in relationships. The study was conducted on six hundred men and women in the US and UK.

It led me to do a little math. The current world population is seven billion. Twenty-six per cent of these are children, and we can presume that they are not sexually active. That leaves us with about 5.18 billion adults. A study based on six hundred people means you have looked at only 0.000011 per cent of the world adult population. What also struck me about this study was that it had not taken into account people from any other countries or cultures, including India, China or any other Asian country, which together account for almost 60 per cent of the world population. Drawing conclusions about the promiscuity of all humans based on a micro-fraction of the population, where you have to count the number of zeroes after the decimal point, without taking into account cultural, socio-economic and other factors that decide who we sleep with behind whose back, might not be a reliable indicator of our propensity to stray. The scientists were quick to declare that human behaviour was influenced by many factors including environment and life experiences.

Most animal species do not mate for life, and are, by default, promiscuous. There is no 'stable relationship' and mating could be a one-time event. Some animals do form a 'pair bond' but there are no restrictions regarding mating outside the pair bond and they copulate with other animals in the group. Humans do it too—except that when one is in a committed relationship, it is shrouded in secrecy for obvious reasons. Everyone wants to have fun but nobody wants to be caught, judged and condemned. I am yet to meet a person who will openly declare that they are promiscuous and be proud of it, unless it is an adolescent bragging to friends that they finally did it and it was 'earth-shattering' and 'mind-blowing', which would probably be far from what it actually was.

If one is to go by evolutionary psychologists, promiscuity is a good thing. It is a tendency that is inherited from our ancestors who hunted for food. Promiscuity multiplied manifold the likelihood of having children and was great for the species from an evolutionary point of view. It also allowed women to choose those men for their offspring, who might have better genes than their partners. For men, it was advantageous as it allowed them to father more children, thus increasing the numbers in their species.

Just because somebody's ring finger is longer than their index finger, it does not mean they will cheat on their spouses. Even if there is some truth in the study, whether one strays from a committed relationship or not depends on many more factors than the length of the fingers. In fact, I would say that for the study results to provide any evidence, one would have to find a substantial number of people who cheated on their partners, measure their ring and index fingers and see if the majority of them had longer ring fingers. This might prove to be an impossible task as nobody would admit to cheating.

I pointed out all the above to Sumana. And then I asked her if she had checked her own fingers. When she did we found out that her left hand was likely to cheat and her right hand was likely to be faithful.

Needless to say, we have never discussed fingers and promiscuity since then.

Are we genetically programmed to stray?

MARRIAGES BREAK UP ALL the time because of infidelity; one such casualty was Rupert Murdoch, who filed for divorce from Wendi Deng after discovering her involvement with former British prime minister Tony Blair.

Dr Christopher Ryan, a PhD of psychology and co-author of the book *Sex at Dawn,* argues that human beings are not built to be monogamous. He says that human beings have not descended from apes—but are apes. He quotes Gerald Durrell who pointed out in one of his books that humans are more closely related to chimps than the Indian elephant is related to the African elephant.

A long time ago, men, women and children lived in groups. Each group had about thirty members and two or three male leaders. Everybody was free to sleep with anyone they desired. The children were all looked after by the women, who stayed back at home and cooked. The men would bring home the food. Gradually, the hunter-gatherers settled down and formed agrarian societies. The harder working and more able-bodied males naturally had an advantage and could claim bigger pieces of land to be cultivated. This gave rise to the need for demarcated property and also the need for more stable arrangements, which sowed the seeds for marriage as an institution.

Back then, its primary purpose was to recognise the legitimate heirs to whom the property could be bequeathed. Once married, a woman became a man's 'possession'. He provided her food and shelter and she, in return, provided him children and the promise of fidelity. In ancient Greece, the father gave away the daughter with the words, 'I pledge my daughter for the purpose of producing legitimate offspring.'

By the eighth century, the Roman Catholic Church got involved and a priest's blessings were needed for the marriage to be legally binding and recognised. In 1563, in the council of Trent, the sacramental nature of marriage was incorporated into the law. Throughout history, not only in India but across all continents, there have been many instances of kings marrying off their daughters to forge new alliances and to expand territories. In ancient times, people married for many reasons, and love was not one of them.

However, this changed gradually as women got more rights, including the right to vote. Women began to be financially independent and began carving their own identities; they were no longer confined to being somebody's daughter or wife. The institution of marriage too evolved slowly into a bond between equals, and a union for love and companionship.

Dr Ryan points out that human beings have been around for two hundred thousand years and agriculture arose only in the last ten thousand, which means that humans have spent only 5 per cent of their time on Earth forced to conform to the diktats of monogamy.

Liaisons outside the marital bed have existed ever since the institution of marriage has, and we have come across thousands of instances of infidelity in books, movies, literature, art and real life. In *Lady Chatterley's Lover* by D.H. Lawrence, Constance, who is married to Clifford Chatterley, has an affair with the gamekeeper Oliver Mellors, risking her marriage, wealth and status. In *Madame Bovary* by Gustave Flaubert, Emma, very disillusioned by the dullness of her marriage, takes a lover and the taxi ride with him through the streets of Rouen in a cab, shielding their illicit relationship from prying eyes, is poignant.

Cheating when you are in a committed relationship has always been a subject of endless fascination, and Indians are not immune to it. Though many movies in India have dealt with the theme, the Bollywood movie *Kabhi Alvida Naa Kehna* had the unsuspecting audience collectively gasping when the lead pair, each married to someone else, was shown having sex with each other. After one recovered from the oh-my-god-they-actually-did-it moment, the camera lingered on their hands, firmly clasped together, their respective wedding bands on, reminding viewers of the lines that had now been blurred, obliterated by the transgression. The film grossed a worldwide total of eighteen million US dollars and was screened over one thousand two hundred cinemas worldwide. Adultery had never been so understood.

In the recent movie *Gone Girl*, adapted from the bestselling book of the same name by Gillian Flynn,

Nick Dunne (played by Ben Affleck) cheats on his beautiful wife Amy (played by Rosamund Pike). Nick, a journalist living in New York, has been laid off and they move back to his home town in North Carthage, Missouri, where he starts teaching journalism in a college. He slowly gets drawn into having an affair with his twenty-three-year-old student. In connection with his extramarital affair, Nick says, 'Love makes you want to be a better man—right, right. But maybe love, real love, also gives you permission to just be the man you are.' Nick feels that he is himself when he is with Andie, his student, whom he is in love with. He laughs a lot, is unguarded and is not bitter and cynical which is the way he is when he is with Amy. About Amy, Nick says that she had many male friends whom she insisted were just friends, but she kept them close enough so they would do her bidding at the crook of a finger, but far enough that Nick couldn't object. The brilliant, dark, suspense-filled story explores the changing dynamics between two people, and—if one reads between the lines—makes a compelling case against marriage. Many people tweeted about losing faith in the institution of marriage after watching the movie.

In an online forum for relationships, a woman confesses that she has been having an affair with her best friend's husband. They are family friends, and their children play together. Though she is burdened with guilt, she is unable to stop. A confession will mean that she loses not only a husband but also a best friend.

Another man in the same forum says that he is married and loves his wife very much. Yet he is attracted to a colleague and has developed a close bond with her. They have also had sex on a few occasions and he now wants to know whether it is possible to love two people with the same intensity.

There are many factors that make a married person or one in a committed relationship cheat. The relationship itself could have changed. There might be issues which were pushed under the rug and never discussed till they grew into a gigantic invisible boulder that crushed the relationship completely. Time could have taken its toll, transforming the ones who fell in love into unrecognisable strangers living under the same roof—masquerading familiarity beneath recognised garbs. But that it could perhaps be biological is not something most people would think. Research now shows though that someone might just be wired to cheat. They cannot help having a propensity to cheat like they can't help having curly hair or being short or having crooked teeth.

When I first came across AVPR1A, I mistakenly read it as 'Av-Priya' and wondered why a gene should be so unusually named, that too, an Indian name with a prefix which makes you think it is a new product promising some dazzling audio-visual features, rather than what is actually is—a gene that determines if you are likely to cheat in your relationships. Researchers in the University of Queensland conducted a study that involved more than seven thousand three hundred twins between the ages of eighteen and forty-nine, all of whom were in a long-term relationship. They compiled data on how many of the subjects had two or more sexual partners in the last one year. They then isolated the identical twins who shared all their genes and the non-identical ones who did not. What they discovered was that unfaithful behaviour in men (63 per cent of the men) and women (a more modest 40 per cent) can be attributed to genes. Women with a certain variant of a gene called AVPR1A—responsible for the hormone that regulates social behaviour—were more likely to be unfaithful.

In a similar study conducted by the State University of New York a few years ago, social scientists discovered that when a man or a woman with this gene has an affair, he or she experiences a surge of dopamine, and it is the same rush that is produced in the case of a gambler whose fortunes have changed in his favour, or an alcoholic who gets that much longed-for drink. These individuals were more likely than others in committed relationships to have a trail of one-night stands and were twice as likely to cheat when compared to individuals who did not possess this gene.

But this does not mean that everyone who is born with this gene will definitely cheat. It does depend a lot on the will-power of the individual and what their value systems are. However, 'Sorry, darling, I can't help it, it's my genes', now seems to be a plausible excuse, scientifically-backed too, when it comes to explaining why you ended up in bed with that oh-so-attractive person you met at the party, even though you were already in a loving relationship.

Maybe Nick Dunne could have used this excuse to tell Amy why he had strayed. Like hundreds of others who have cheated on their partners and yet have chosen to remain in the relationship, their partners blissfully unaware of the deep dark secrets buried under the happy smiles.

But the day it all comes out will be the day of reckoning and whether your partner chooses to forgive you or not will be another story.

A marriage is a long road and everyone makes the commitment with the promise of happily-ever-after. But whether the happily-ever-after lasts or gets plagued by mistrust, jealousies, temptation and other distractions is anybody's guess.

Love may last forever and ever, but sometimes the partner changes.

Affairs in the workplace

IN 1989, IN A law firm in Chicago, a young man, a summer intern, asked his mentor out. She turned him down but he was persistent. She finally relented, and they watched a movie together on their first date. Three years later they were engaged. They got married the following year, and are married to date. The pair was none other than Michelle and Barack Obama. This is perhaps one of the most famous workplace romances that led to the altar. There are other equally well-known couples, like Bill and Melinda Gates, Angelina Jolie and Brad Pitt, and Aamir Khan and Kiran Rao—if you want a couple who are closer home—who met at work.

More often than not there is nothing official about office romances. Once Cupid strikes, you tend to linger longer at water coolers, coffee vending machines or the photocopying area, depending on where you are likely to run into your object of interest. If you happen to work on the same project together, chances are you will be passing 'You look awesome' and 'Meet me for a cup of coffee?' notes discreetly—or not so discreetly, depending on how alert your colleagues are—during boring company meetings.

Given the extra-long working hours which demanding careers require and the kind of amenities that most modern-day offices interested in retaining talent flaunt, right from fully-equipped gyms, cafeterias and snooker tables, it is no surprise that offices are fertile grounds for relationships to bloom. After all, here is a large selection pool where you are likely to meet someone who has a similar background and educational qualifications and a lot more in common than anyone you would meet on a matrimonial site (if your intentions are to get married) or a dating site (no matter what your intentions are or your marital status is).

Sometimes, even when people are in committed relationships, there develops an affinity for a certain co-worker. This has given rise to a new phenomenon called 'office spouse'. It is an American term that has been coined to describe a relationship that develops between members who work in close proximity with each other for long hours. There is an unwritten understanding between the two that they will be there for each other throughout their careers, providing support from a demanding boss, impossible deadlines, unbearable colleagues or targets that are higher than the combined heights of Mount Everest and Kangchenjunga.

One may or may not be romantically involved with the office spouse. The relationship may be platonic, but there is a very real chance of it developing into a full-blown affair. When two colleagues work closely enough, they face similar pressures, deadlines and targets. They have a couple of meals together and slowly start sharing stuff that is personal. The line between official and personal gradually blurs over messages exchanged on BBMs and WhatsApp. They become clever, funny and border on the slightly flirtatious, without really crossing any lines. Time spent with the co-worker suddenly seems fun, especially when you have to go back home after a long, hard day to discuss children's report cards, mundane domestic chores or due dates of electricity bills. Your co-worker probably understands you more than your spouse does, because your spouse just doesn't grasp what you face at work. The emotional connect happens slowly (after all, it is not like you are having a relationship; hey—this is just a co-worker, remember), and before one realises, it has transformed into a full-blown physical affair.

To have an affair at work is a huge risk as it damages your reputation. Even if the affair does not really impact your work, chances are it will not be viewed that way. When someone is at work, they seem more alluring as they are doing something that they are naturally good at. While minor flirtations are inevitable and perhaps break the drudgery of long hours, anything that goes beyond it is a cause for concern. If you get into an affair with the person you are reporting to, then it can have serious repercussions.

Many corporate offices have a policy on workplace romances. While some companies don't have a problem as long as the two are not in the same department, other companies have clauses that require employees to declare any such relationship if it develops during the tenure of employment. The reason is not hard to figure. If a manager gets involved with a subordinate, it would be hard to rule out favouritism. Between two people in the same department too, it could lead to distractions that affect work.

For some reason, if things fall apart and the couple breaks up, it is going to be very hard to see each other on a daily basis. If you have to work with them after the relationship ends, it is going to be a difficult task to keep emotions at bay and carry on as though nothing has happened.

If you decide to embark on an office romance, as unromantic and clinical as it might sound, it is always wise to check the company policy on the same before throwing your heart in. Whether it leads to marriage, unemployment or divorce is something that only time will tell.

BETWEEN THE SHEETS

Sex is a part of nature. I go along with nature.

–Marilyn Monroe

Sex is kicking death in the ass while singing.

–Charles Bukowski

Would you sleep with someone for money?

IN THE 1993 MOVIE *Indecent Proposal*, multi-millionaire John Gage (played by Robert Redford) offers one million dollars to a couple, for him to spend the night with the wife Diana (played by the stunning Demi Moore). He does not mention sex at all, but that is what she presumes it involves. She is very much in love with her architect husband, and though not wealthy, their love—sometimes cloyingly, annoyingly perfect—more than makes up for anything they lack materialistically. Recession hits them hard and they go to Las Vegas to try and make up for their losses in a casino, but the gamble they take proves to be the ultimate one—it turns out to be a gamble on their relationship. The aftermath of that one night which she spends with the millionaire forms the rest of the movie. It is a tug between love, lust and the very real offer of a million dollars. The story might be fictional but the fact that it was a huge box office success, crossing 266 million US dollars worldwide, shows that the sanctity of a marriage versus the love of money is a theme which strikes a chord with many and makes people think.

The Austin Institute for the Study of Family and Culture strives to explain the economics of sex, laying bare the reality of relationships in economic terms. It asks us to think of sex as an exchange where each person gives the other person something of themselves—i.e., intimate access to each other's bodies, which they both enjoy. While on face value, it seems like they are both giving each other the same thing, it is not really so. It goes on to explain that, on an average, men have a higher sex drive than women because of testosterone, and so men initiate sex more than women. They are also more sexually permissive than women, and they connect sex to romance less often than women. It asserts that women, in contrast to men, have sex for reasons far beyond simple physical pleasure. A woman would have sex to fulfil her needs for expressing and receiving love. She would also have sex to strengthen commitment or affirm her desirability. The study goes on to explain why marriage rates are dropping but online dating is increasing.

In *Fifty Shades of Grey*, the hot topic of discussion that raises not just libido but also tempers—for there are many who don't like the book—is that it would be difficult to imagine Ms Steele agreeing to do all that she did with Mr Grey had he been a little less rich than what he was. She was fascinated that someone so wealthy would find her attractive and did not think twice before hopping into his private plane, which transported her to an alternate reality involving ropes and other things she had not remotely thought she would be associated with.

Did she walk out and refuse to be his submissive slave, though she knew it involved harm to her? No—she obliged excitedly as her 'inner goddess' kept jumping up and down, urging her to go ahead and indulge in a little adventure. What made it easier for her, apart from his money, was his good looks. What if he looked like a toad, warts and all, and yet offered her diamond-studded handcuffs and a whip with a handle decorated with precious stones as a takeaway memento of their not-so-innocent encounter? Would she have accepted? Whether she would have slapped him and walked out or whether she would have grinned and said yes is a question for debate. If we are to go by popular culture and popular opinion, women seem a lot more tolerant to atrocious offers made by good-looking men!

Which brings us to a pertinent question: what would *you* do for a million dollars? Would you sleep with someone? I am yet to meet a man who will not be tempted by this offer, no matter what a woman looks like. But for a woman, the answer to that question would probably be, 'If it were someone as attractive as Robert Redford or George Clooney, I would sleep with him for free.'

Do women really want muscular men?

MANY YEARS AGO, I attended a party on Women's Day where no men were allowed. It was at a posh hotel in the city and the special event of the day was a ramp walk. I presumed it would be the usual fashion show where skinny models showed off haute couture outfits which you could never wear on a daily basis, unless you wanted to create an impression that you were on your way to a costume party. To my surprise, the people who walked down the ramp were not lanky women, but muscular, well-built men, oozing testosterone, dressed in boxers, briefs and G-strings, every muscle in their body pumped up as though they had just stepped out of the gym between reps. The cheer that went up was ear-shattering as the huge group of women whistled, hooted and shouted their appreciation. The men were all sportive about it, acknowledging the compliments gracefully by winking and smiling. They were clearly enjoying the attention. I watched in amusement as the gender roles were reversed that night. I secretly wondered how many hours the guys on the ramp must have spent at the gym to achieve the bodies they were proudly flaunting.

So, how much do women really care about muscles on a man? Several scientific studies around the world consistently say the same thing: that women are indeed drawn to a guy who is muscular when it comes to brief flings or one-night stands. Nobody is looking for someone who makes compelling conversation when the objective is short-term fun. Also, most women do not size up men with the same competitive eye that men have while sizing each other up. If the guy is reasonably fit, a woman will not really care about whether he has four-pack abs or a six-pack. When it comes to choosing a mate, women get pickier. They are likely to choose the guy who will be a good provider and a good husband even if he has a less than perfect body.

A 2012 study by the University of Westminster says that men who are obsessed with building muscles are significantly likely to objectify women, be hostile towards them, and are likely to be sexist. The study says that these men are also likely to find thinner women more attractive. For the purpose of the study, the researchers had surveyed a group of 327 heterosexual British men out of which 38 per cent were single, 31 per cent were in a relationship, 23 per cent were married and the rest were in the 'other' category. There were many articles that popped up on the basis of this study which said that muscular men made the worst boyfriends for it would be awful to be in a relationship with them and women would do better if they picked the scrawny guy.

The study included only a small sample size, that too from one single country and drew conclusions about muscular men in general. The fact is culture, belief, value system, level of education, exposure and degree of open-mindedness is what will influence anybody's attitude towards life in general and the other gender in particular, whether they are muscular or not.

A person who is muscular and fit has achieved that by putting in a lot of hard work and many hours at the gym. Building muscle requires a certain degree of commitment. We don't need a study to tell us that if a person is fit, then he or she is definitely disciplined, consistent, perseverant and is willing to work hard to get results—all qualities which can lead to a great relationship, provided the guy is not self-obsessed and narcissistic, which is a charge that most men who are into building muscles face.

Also, a woman who keeps herself fit is likely to be drawn to a guy who is the same. So if the muscular guy shows a preference for women who are thin, it would not be fair to label him sexist. He is merely finding a quality that he himself has being reflected in a woman and is drawn to her because of that quality. It would be akin to an intelligent guy being attracted to a really smart woman or a guy who likes hiking being drawn to a girl who likes hiking too, which is hardly sexist.

When it comes to muscles, the women seem unanimous in their verdict. A little eye candy is great but if you want to be in it for the long haul, there better be some depth to the personality too.

Sex and the Indian woman

'The language of sex is sexist. A man "takes" a woman. A woman "gives herself" to a man. But there are things men and women do equally well—stalking, pining, texting, dumping,' said my friend and fellow author Shinie Antony to me, at the Bangalore Times Litfest 2015. Our session was called 'Sex on Toast', and we were discussing all things related to sex and society and how sex is portrayed in literature.

I pointed out that there were many derogatory terms to describe a woman who did not conform to society's idea of how she should behave sexually. There are words like whore, slut and bitch to describe a woman who is perceived as sexually promiscuous. But when a man does the same, he is a stud, a Romeo or a ladies' man. Our culture is skewed in favour of men when it comes to sex. The message that society sends out clearly takes an undertone of 'boys will be boys' and 'good girls will never do that' when it comes to expressing oneself sexually. People are more forgiving of a man who strays, while a woman who does the same is not so easily let off the hook.

According to a recently conducted sex survey by India Today-MDRA, 77 per cent of Indian men still want their brides to be virgins. Also thrice the number of men as women admitted to having premarital sex. The question arises then as to who these men are having sex with, if their numbers are three times that of women. It clearly means that they are either having sex with other men, or visiting brothels, or that the women have multiple partners—or the most likely explanation, i.e., far fewer women admit to actually having premarital sex because of the diktats of 'being a good Indian girl'.

So what then is this 'good Indian girl' expected to do? If we are to go by the ads and the movies, she being a modern woman is expected to give orders at the office and handle everything her male colleagues do, and then she is expected to come home and get dinner ready. And then there are 'progressive' advertisements too. An ad for a bag shows a girl waking up next to a guy in a men's hostel and running out draped only in a bed sheet. She then gets dressed in a loose T-shirt and shorts while on the move. Then there is an ad showing a woman getting married for a second time, with her daughter looking on. There are ads for a sanitary napkin that show women as pilots, in the army, in office and playing a sport. Women are portrayed as strong and independent, free to pursue their goals.

However, the fact that these ads get talked about indicate that they are in the minority. Also most of these ads depict young, unmarried (or about to be married) women. Traditional ads still show women in the role of a homemaker, fondly serving her family. It seems as though the message being sent out is that a woman can do what she wants before marriage, but after marriage, she better 'settle down' and take care of the family.

In a country where the female infanticide rate is amongst the highest in the world, where we lose three million girls in infanticide in the span of a decade, the need of the hour is to stop treating a woman as a mere sex object. Our society needs to recognise that a woman is much more than how beautiful she is (when unmarried) or how she can turn into a martyr for her family once she is married.

Our bawdy song lyrics objectify women, comparing them to a 'tandoori chicken', among other things. At family weddings, lyrics that celebrate the posterior of a woman are played loudly, stating that 'all the boys go crazy when I shake my…'. Our country sees nothing wrong in that and anyone protesting is told to lighten up—it is only a joke and should be taken in a lighter vein.

But as long as the attitude of hypocrisy prevails, and as long as women are still expected to be 'good girls' suppressing their sexual needs, putting everyone else before them, this treatment of women will continue. If we are to truly progress, we need to look at women differently, and respect their needs. A truly liberated woman is one who is comfortable enough with her sexuality and who doesn't have to shake any body part to prove that she is sexy.

What your sleeping position says about your relationship

According to my spouse, I do not occupy my side of the bed at all. I move over to his side and stick to him, forcing him to occupy just 10 per cent of the bed while the remainder is left empty. He never fails to mention it, but the way he talks about it, I know he secretly loves it. It's a joke between us now.

'So you planning to sleep on my side again?' he asks.

'What your side? You didn't read the fine print when you got married to me. You signed off all bed-occupancy rights,' I retort and he chuckles.

We have got used to each other's sleep habits now.

A cartoon by Cathy Thorne shows a couple together in bed, with one of them awake sitting up in bed and the other snoring happily, an air-conditioner in the background, and a caption that reads, 'Couples should sleep together as early as possible—only to find out if they are bedroom-temperature compatible'.

Any couple who has been in a long-term relationship can vouch for the adjustments that have to be made in the bedroom after the other parameters of compatibility, like values, intellect and that physical connect have been ticked, and the relationship is on its way to a 'happily committed' status, from the initial let's-see-where-it-leads stage.

Chances are that if one wants to work in bed, the other will complain about the clackety-clack of the keyboard and will fine-tune the grumbling to a crescendo, till the offending laptop is switched off. If one wants to read in bed and the other wants to sleep, the light has to be adjusted in such a manner as to illuminate only the book and not the partner's face.

Finally when the couple settles down to sleep, they settle into their favourite sleeping positions. During sleep you cannot fake your body language and this is the time when one is most honest and vulnerable. Scientists have conducted studies to decipher what sleeping positions say about the relationship of a couple. If there is a change in the dynamics of the relationship, then it affects the sleeping position too as it is usually reflective of what is happening between them.

If a couple sleeps with their backs to each other, but yet touch each other, it means that they are comfortable, intimate and relaxed with each other. If they sleep back to back and do not touch, it means they are independent in their relationship, are used to each other and accept each other. Based on a study conducted for the Edinburgh Science Festival, which surveyed about thousand people, it was found that 42 per cent of people lie back to back, 31 per cent face the same direction and only 4 per cent face each other.

If they sleep in the spooning position, with the man on the outside and the woman on the inside, it indicates a traditional role where the guy protects and takes care of the woman, and she allows him to. If this is reversed—that is, the woman is on the outside—then it indicates that the woman takes the lead in protecting the man. Less than 5 per cent of couples sleep this way.

If the couple sleeps facing each other, but don't touch each other, it means they feel the need for more intimacy and more conversation in their relationship. If they sleep facing each other with legs intertwined all night, then it means that they cannot bear to be separated even for a moment. Young lovers are most likely to adopt this position.

The study concluded that it was possible to tell how happy a couple is in a relationship by measuring the distance between them when they sleep. They discovered that the happiest couples were those who touched each other while they slept, as compared to the ones that preferred not to touch. The study also concluded that partners who slept less than an inch apart were more likely to be content with their relationship than those who maintained a gap of thirty inches or more.

The popular Hollywood movie posture, where the woman lies with her head on the man's chest, is adopted by just 1 per cent of couples. While it makes a great shot for a movie, it usually ends up with a cramped arm in real life, and not many men, no matter how much they love their woman, are willing to do that.

If the woman sprawls out on the bed like a starfish, occupying most of the space, with the guy practically hanging off the bed, it means that she is likely to want her space in the relationship and the man is happy to let her have it. If the roles are reversed and the guy occupies most of the bed, with the woman taking a small bit of it, then it indicates that he likes to have his way in the relationship and she is happy to oblige.

So, there is more to a good night's sleep than meets the eye and if you stick like a leech to your partner, it is likely that your love will cling on too.

How important is sex in a relationship?

'NOT TONIGHT, DEAR, I have a headache', is a phrase much touted, much maligned and perhaps a bit too stereotypical, existing from a time when withholding sex was used as a weapon, perpetuating the myth of the horny husband and the frigid wife. In today's times, it could be either one or both of the partners not wanting action between the sheets and instead preferring to put up their feet on the centre table, open a bottle of beer or wine as the case may be and watch television at the end of a hard, stressful day.

In today's busy world, where people juggle careers, deadlines and traffic jams that come with city-living and kids—if they have any—what gets compromised is the time that they spend with each other. With many distractions such as the smartphone and internet, the quality of time that the couple spends together takes a drastic hit. Sex then becomes a chore to be performed at the end of a long day. More so when the couple has been with each other for a while: it gets bumped down in the list of priorities. For most women, conversation, mood and a little romance is needed to kindle the fire of desire. But the modern-day lifestyle with so much multi-tasking affords only a compressed version of the above. Sex, or the lack of it, becomes the elephant in the room; no one talks about it, and it slowly begins to take a toll on the relationship.

In a study in Australia, researchers interviewed about three thousand two hundred men and three thousand three hundred women who were either married or in a relationship, and living with their partners for over ten years. Fifty-four per cent of the men, and 42 per cent of the women interviewed said they were unhappy with the frequency of sex in their relationship.

One of the partners might desire more sex, but the other might be too busy or too stressed. Lack of physical intimacy—for genuine reasons, whatever they may be—creates a gap in a relationship through which other issues creep in. Sometimes they are in the guise of infidelity—where the partner who would like more intimacy seeks it outside the relationship. Sometimes they are in other forms such as seeking refuge in alcohol, drugs, comfort-eating or excessive time spent on social media. It becomes a vicious circle and the couple drifts apart. The relationship between them weakens slowly, without them even realising it, and when they finally do, a lot of damage has already been wreaked. If the gap has grown too large, it eventually results in a break-up. That the bottled-up resentment could stem from a lack of sex is a reason not often considered.

In case a couple has grown apart sexually, they need to analyse why it has happened. Is one of the partners constantly making excuses? What is that issue that is causing stress in the relationship, which results in the sex life waning? A little examination and introspection by both parties will throw up answers and solutions. The key here is honesty. Once the issues are out in the open, they would then need to make changes accordingly, if they want their sex lives to improve.

Many experts recommend setting aside a specific time for sex, just as one sets aside time for dental appointments, as drab and boring as it may sound. Films and media always depict characters in the throes of passion, ripping each other's clothes off as if they cannot withhold their desire any longer. But sex in real life need not always be that way. Sex need not be spontaneous, wild and passionate for it to be great. If a couple values the sex in their relationship, they have to make it a priority. Open communication with each other and expressing what you need helps. Couples have to discuss what works for them, how many times they would like to do it, and then reach an understanding.

Sex plays an important role in relationships and if the sexual chemistry is great and other parameters are met, then the bond which emerges is stronger than in a relationship which scores a tick-mark in all departments except sex.

Sex binds—but only if you both love it equally.

What does consent mean when it comes to sex?

UNDERSTANDING CONSENT IS NOT hard. It just means that the individual is agreeing to do—or refrain from doing—certain things. It could be implied consent—for example, when you enrol in an educational institution, you automatically agree to abide by the rules of that institution. It could also be a written consent—for example, in a medical procedure, where you sign documents saying that you are aware of the risks involved. When it comes to sexual consent, both parties have to be adult and have a clear verbal communication or non-verbal agreement that both do want to have sex and are engaging in it fully aware of what they are doing. Violation of this consent would be termed sexual assault.

The question that arises is how do we treat drunken sex? What if the woman seemed eager for it when drunk, and the next morning has no clue of anything that transpired the previous night? She might have given her consent earlier in the evening, but what if she cries rape now? How does one understand clearly what consent is?

Sometime back a brilliant video explaining sexual consent with the help of stick figures and a cup of tea went viral. It explained sexual consent in the most simple way, where they equated having sex with somebody making a cup of tea for them. The video explained that when you ask someone if they want tea, they might say yes enthusiastically and then you can be sure that they do want it and you could proceed to make tea for them. On the other hand, they may say that they are not sure, in which case you could make them a cup of tea, but you have to be aware that they may not drink it. Sometimes, they might have said yes to a cup of tea, but in the time that it took for you to make the cup of tea, they might have changed their mind. If they did, you have to respect their choice—you can't pour tea down their throats or force them to have it. Also, just because they said yes to tea last Saturday, it doesn't mean they want it every day of the week and you certainly cannot turn up at their place with a cup of tea, expecting them to drink it, because they had once said yes to tea with you.

The video also went on to emphasise that if someone was unconscious, it was completely not acceptable to pour tea down their throats—unconscious people do not want tea—a reference to sex with someone who is so drunk that they have passed out.

Many people think that if a woman sends mixed signals it is okay for the man to 'cajole her', the cajoling being loosely defined as anything between pinning her down and trying to kiss her or him gripping her tightly and telling her that he loves her while begging her for a kiss. A woman might have complimented a guy, gone out for a couple of drinks with him and even invited him home for a cup of coffee. But that doesn't mean she has said yes, yet. If he tries to initiate sex and she refuses or says she isn't ready, it means she just isn't ready. If the man thinks that he can get her to change her mind by acting like a Mills & Boon hero—the macho guy, the alpha male who just takes his women and has his way with them, while the women flutter their eyelashes and fall in love with him—he is mistaken. Real life doesn't work that way. She might be put off by the stubble on his chin which he feels is sexy but she thinks is like sandpaper. Or she might be put off by his presumption that she doesn't really know what she wants. Or she just might be put off by his lack of respect for her feelings. Either way, if she says no, she means no, and she isn't asking for it.

It is the same for men. Just because a woman is dying to have sex with a man she fancies, it doesn't mean he would want to reciprocate. The notion that men never say no to free sex is false.

When it is between two consenting adults, sex can be fun, enjoyable and can take people to heights they never imagined before, depending on how skilled the lovers are. But when there is force, nothing can be a greater put-off. The video sums it up well, when it says, 'Whether it is tea or sex, consent is everything.'

What's your dirtiest fantasy?

'WHAT IS YOUR DIRTIEST fantasy?' asks a wide-eyed Meg Ryan looking directly into Alec Baldwin's eyes, unblinking, probing and not breaking away her gaze in the 1992 movie *Prelude to a Kiss*. He wonders if he heard right and manages to splutter out an 'Excuse me?' She repeats the question. He initially says he cannot tell her. But she insists. And then he reveals it.

Sexual fantasies are a universal phenomenon. In some cultures, people openly talk about it, whereas in others it is suppressed. In 1973, it was believed that only men had sexual fantasies. A popular women's magazine known for encouraging women to express themselves sexually had an article that year with the headline: 'Women don't have sexual fantasies, period. Men do.' We have come a long way since then and the same magazine now asserts that women enjoy sex as much as men and tells them to show guys where their G-spot is.

In a survey, it was found that common women's sexual fantasies included dominating a strong man begging for sexual release in the bedroom, being dominated by a guy who pins her down and has his way with her, teacher-student role play where she dresses up as a school girl and gets spanked, a no-strings attached one-night stand, and a threesome with two men who adore and worship her. Men's sexual fantasies included cheating, cleavage sex, watching a partner masturbate, sex with strangers, being a voyeur watching a woman undress and a threesome with two women (but of course!).

Since the process of a fantasy is entirely imaginary and it comes from deep in the psyche, someone who has a wild fantasy might be mortified if you suggested that they could enact it in real life. Researchers have always known that sexual fantasies tell us a lot about the person, but just how much they reveal has been a journey of ongoing discussion and new discoveries, keeping those research wheels busily whirring even as couples enact what they most want or suppress it for fear of rebuke and scorn from their partner. What they share with each other depends on how open their partner is to trying new things, and their comfort level in the bedroom—that one place where you are at your most vulnerable.

A fascinating study of sexual fantasies by an Israeli psychologist, Gurit E. Birnbaum, discovered that sexual fantasies of a couple or an individual reveal not only personality traits and their attachment patterns to people but also how they relate to each other. We all have different attachment styles and different needs in a relationship.

He may want to be in constant communication while she might feel the need to communicate only every few days. She might expect him to be more vocal in his expression of love for her, but his way of showing love might be ensuring that the electricity bills are paid on time and reminding her of her dentist's appointment because he knows she will forget.

It was also found that both men and women fantasise equally, and two-third of the participants fantasised about their partner. However, only 50 per cent of the men's fantasies involved their partner as against 83 per cent of the women. The content of their fantasies were also very different. The fantasies that emerged were grouped into expressions of attachment anxiety or avoidance. People who had high avoidance traits had fantasies of aggression, which emotionally distanced them from their mate. People who had anxious attachment traits had fantasies that involved being comforted and held when they felt that their relationship was being threatened. Anxiously attached people also had fantasies of completely surrendering control to their partner and being humiliated and helpless in the hands of a very powerful partner. Birnbaum's study seems to suggest that understanding your sexual fantasies and analysing them might prove to be a valuable tool to understanding yourself and your need for intimacy.

In the movie that I mentioned, Meg Ryan proceeds to make his fantasy come true and he screams in pleasure. Now if that happened a lot more in real life, we would have a lot of sexually-content people basking in the warm glow of a post-coital cuddle with a silly grin on their faces, telling each other, 'You're the best, baby,' and actually meaning it.

Nothing beats good sex when it comes to forming a strong connect. And sometimes the lines of fantasy and reality blur, making it the greatest high ever.

Sex and the Indian teen

AT A STAND-UP COMEDY show that I attended in my city, the performer was surprised to see a man in the audience with his fourteen-year-old daughter. The performer asked the man if he knew what Tinder was and the man admitted he did not. When he asked the daughter she smiled, nodded and looked away, and the stand-up comedian told her not to tell her father. The audience burst into laughter at this exchange, and as I joined in, I thought about how reflective it was of the times we live in. A majority of parents aren't tech-savvy and most would not be using half the apps that their smartphones flaunt. They come from a generation where showing tender loving care in a relationship was more important than having Tinder in your smartphone for a 'relationship of a different kind' and where Cupids were not okay until after marriage.

When we were growing up, our parents liked to pretend that sex didn't exist. A biology class would be the only place where it would be talked about by a stern-faced teacher who threw up terms like acrosome, interstitial cells and the processes that took place which facilitated the sperm to penetrate the egg. All our knowledge—in the absence of the internet—was gleaned from older friends who told us very knowledgeably that the sperm can enter the body through the mouth when you kissed a guy after which it swam through your oesophagus to penetrate the egg and we believed them. Contrast this to the current generation—born after 1996, when the internet first came to India, the know-it-alls who have never heard of a dial-up connection—and they will tell you that sex is fun, a cool thing to do, but you better be careful and use protection. They will also tell you that good grades are more important than sex, and virginity is for the 'ancient times'.

The India-Today sex survey of 2014 throws up some startling numbers: 3 out of 10 students of Class X are not virgins, 22 per cent have had sex with relatives, 26 per cent are into sexting, and 71 per cent have had their first sexual encounters at home—either theirs or somebody else's. In the metros, 47 per cent know somebody who got pregnant as a teen. While the numbers show that today's young person is exploring his or her sexuality and experimenting like never before, some things never change: 91 per cent of teens do not speak to their parents about sex and 70 per cent of them are not allowed to have a boyfriend or a girlfriend.

Against the above numbers, I can only imagine the peer pressure that exists for a teen today. If all their friends are into sexting and using Snapchat, if it is the 'cool thing to do', it will be very hard to refuse to participate. 'If most of my friends do it, it must be okay,' will be the natural conclusion teens draw, especially in the absence of freedom to talk about it with their parents.

Sex and the Indian teen

Sex is all around us—in television adverts, movies, music videos, on the internet, in magazines—and it is used to sell almost every single thing right from batteries to refrigerators, from washing machines to smartphones. We live in an age of hyper-sexuality where we now have apps to track how many times you did it, what was the level of satisfaction you felt, the exact number of minutes in foreplay and the positions you used. It is no longer a taboo to talk about it, a case in point being the recent video that went viral on social media where young girls in Delhi were asked about masturbation and they openly talked about it without being coy or shy.

But what is important to remember is while a teen may jump right in and do it—one more tick-mark in the list of adults things to do—it might be just a shallow imitation of something deeply powerful which happens only when it is between two consenting adults in a bond that is intensely emotional, involves commitment with the certainty of a meaningful relationship where you are there for each other, growing together as individuals.

That comes only with age and maturity. And there is no app to track the depth of a relationship that has grown over the years and the heights it takes you to.

What turns you on?

A FEW MONTHS AGO a visual I posted on Tumblr showed a guy with only his hands visible, reading a book with a stack of other books piled up next to him. The caption read, 'A man who reads is such a turn-on'. Because the post got a large number of shares, I was curious to know if all women felt the same and hence conducted a little experiment where I forwarded it to many women—some of whom read a lot and some who did not. Most of the non-readers couldn't connect with the visual while the readers nodded their heads in agreement, vouching it was true. What was a turn-on for some women did not make even the slightest impact on others. For women there isn't one universal thing which does it for them. However, for men it is a different story.

For a straight man, a voluptuously sexy woman wearing a bikini and high heels is likely to be a turn on and even if it isn't, he would definitely turn to take a second look. In case he was looking only for sex, he wouldn't care if she had an IQ of 140 and above or not as long he had her phone number.

But when the roles are reversed you would get a picture with a stark contrast. I can state with a fair amount of certainty that if you ask a woman whether a guy in tight swimming trunks and bulges in all the right places turns them on or whether they will pick a smart and witty conversationalist who makes them feel like a million dollars, chances are nine out of ten women will pick the conversationalist. A cartoon captures it well, when it shows a woman driving a car trying to pick up a male prostitute and him saying, 'Oh yeah baby—I will listen to you, I will listen to you all night long'. Most of my married women friends could relate to that one.

Research on women's sexuality indicates that the turn-on factors for women are very different from those for men. In a survey conducted by a magazine, it was found that for women the biggest turn-ons were the thoughtfulness and sensitivity of the guy as opposed to his muscles and biceps. Rehearsed pick-up lines, no matter how clever, were not rated sexy at all as they showed neither his originality nor his intelligence. Instead, what counted as sexy was a sense of humour—additional points if he could make her laugh—an ability to listen, and showing compassion. People who were creative achievers also found intellectual curiosity immensely sexy. When it came to physical attributes, while some women rated a paunch or a beer-belly as a no-no, most said that if the guy had a great personality then a little belly fat would be forgiven, and in fact, they preferred larger men to skinny ones. In another study published in *Evolution and Human Behaviour*, it was found that women were also attracted to a five-day stubble.

All the above findings bring us to the all-important question: aren't women turned on by visual stimuli at all? Is the sex appeal of a man all based on his actions and how he behaves around a woman rather than by what he looks like? Also, are women turned on by porn as much as men are?

Meredith Chivers, a psychology professor at Queens University, a highly regarded scientist and a member of the editorial board of *Archives of Sexual Behaviour*, conducted a series of experiments over the past several years to ascertain what turns on women. When women were shown a variety of porn clips of sex between two women, two men, two chimps mating and a ripped naked man walking, what did not turn on the women was the naked man. They were turned on by everything else in varying degrees. When Chivers tried the same experiment with men, straight men were aroused when there were women on the screen and not at all aroused when men were on the screen.

When it comes to women, clearly there are no correct answers as to what turns her on. It could be his smile, his intellect, his stubble or simply the way he helps around the house.

To please a man is easy. To please a woman is like the Facebook relationship status that reads 'It's complicated'.

How erotica differs from porn

MOST PEOPLE USE FACEBOOK to make a personal statement of who they are and what they stand for. Happy pictures of their holidays, children's achievements, pets, a new home bought, and even what they just had for lunch or dinner are splashed with equal aplomb and pride. The most important thing perhaps for most people using Facebook is their display picture.

Facebook has a strict policy against obscenity and any picture that contains nudity, sexually suggestive content, self-harm, excessive violence or hate speech is promptly removed. A French primary school teacher Frederic Durand-Baissas, a father of three, recently found himself at the receiving end of the censorship when he found his profile blocked for obscenity. Outraged, he took Facebook to court. He had used Gustave Courbet's painting, which everybody—without any age restrictions—can admire at the Musée d'Orsay in Paris, as his display picture. The painting shows the close up of a woman's genitalia and is titled, 'Origin of the World'.

Durand-Baissas demanded twenty thousand euros to be awarded to him as damages, and said that

Zuckerberg's company had no right to censor his account for sharing a masterpiece. Facebook argued that the case should be heard in California, as all users sign a clause while opening an account in the site, which specifies jurisdiction in case of legal action. However, the Paris high court termed the clause abusive and retained the right for French judges to decide the case. Durand-Baisass's lawyer hailed the ruling as a triumph of David against Goliath.

Gustave Courbet, the artist whose painting is in the eye of the storm, was a French painter who pioneered the Realist movement in the nineteenth century. He believed in painting only what he could see. He did not believe in romanticism, which artists before him had embraced. Courbet was a rebel who went against set norms. He painted peasants and workers on a grand scale and this was previously done only for paintings of historical or religious importance. He was arrested for his involvement with the Paris Commune and lived in exile in Switzerland till he died. That he was entirely a free spirit, unshackled by tradition, conventions or what people thought of him, is evident from his famous words: 'I am fifty years old and I have always lived in freedom; let me end my life free; when I am dead let this be said of me—"He belonged to no school, to no church, to no institution, to no academy, least of all to any regime except the regime of liberty".'

One of Courbet's most well-known paintings, 'Young Ladies on the Bank of the Seine', depicts two prostitutes resting under a tree by the river. Till then, art critics had only seen timeless nude women in landscapes, and the entire art community was shocked by the portrayal of two modern women, casually lounging, displaying their undergarments. There is another titled 'Sleep', a beautiful work that shows two nude women in bed. Courbet's work also included stunning landscapes, portraits of various people and also pictures of the working class, including farmers and stone breakers. However, the ones that earned him fame—or notoriety, depending on how conservative the viewer is—were his erotic work.

Michelangelo's famous sculpture David is a marble statue of a nude male. It is a masterpiece that has been reproduced many times. The plaster cast of David that hangs at Victoria and Albert Museum in London has a detachable plastic fig leaf which is displayed nearby. The fig leaf was created in response to Queen Victoria's shock upon first seeing the statue, and it is now hung on the figure prior to visits from members of the royal family, using two strategically-placed hooks.

The thing about art is that there is a fine line between erotica and pornography. Art is highly interpretive. The difference between erotica and pornography is that the former doesn't appeal *exclusively* to our carnal senses. There is more to it than mere titillation and nudity just for the sake of voyeuristic urges. Eroticism has a kind of beauty which is alluring and is provocative in a tasteful manner, engaging our aesthetic senses.

But as long as there are people shocked by nudity, there will continue to be debates on what is permissible and what is not permissible. What is erotic in one's eyes might be pornographic in another's. It just depends on how you see it.

Acknowledgements

ALMOST EVERYONE WE MEET influences us in some way. The impact that some people have on us stays with us for a long time. Some evaporate without a trace. And some teach us lessons.

I have been fortunate to make a connection with thousands of readers through my books, and hence a grateful thanks to all of you who wrote to me, sharing your stories, and also to all of you who read me. Really grateful for all the love.

Thanks to my dad, K.V.J. Kamath, who was solely responsible for instilling in me a love for books. And to my mom, Priya Kamath, with whom I discuss all my book ideas.

Thanks to my wonderful family—Satish, Atul and Purvi, and Lostris too. My life would have been a huge void but for them.

A big thank you to Shinie Antony for her compliments about my writing and without whom 'Sex and the City' would have never happened. Thanks to Manjul Mishra and Shubrangshu Roy too.

Thanks to my friends Vani Mahesh, Mayank Mittal, Anukul Shenoy, Shabina Bhatti, Rathipriya and Suresh Sanyasi for all the support. Much appreciated!

An extra-large dose of thanks to Deepthi Talwar for her skilled editing. She is easily the best editor I have worked with.

Also, thanks to:

~ Sushma and Pradeep Shenoy, who let me use their beautiful home, which was where most of this book took shape.

~ My early readers Avantika Srivastava, Anuttera Pandit, Saurabh Thakral and Basila Ali, who gave me honest feedback and tons of encouragement.

~ My women friends Jayashree Chinne, Priya Selva, Dipa Padmakumar, Vinoo John, Suma Rao, Haritha Venkatrangan, Naaz Pansare and Nishu Mathur. We may not meet as often as I would like, but we always pick up where we left off.

~ My friends from the writing world—Nikita Singh, Kiran Manral, Sachin Garg, Durjoy Datta, Meghna Pant, Nandita Bose and Milan Vohra.

~ J.K Bose and Arup Bose for that first yes.

~ Narasimha Murthy who clicked brilliant photos of me.

~ Pranav Shah for my website.

~ And finally, Manju and Ramakrishna, who make my life easier by saving me loads of time.

About the author

Preeti Shenoy, one of India's most popular authors, has written sixteen bestselling titles and her books have sold over a million copies. Known for her accessible writing style, she tackles complex themes like mental health, gender inequality and socio-economic divides. Preeti has been featured on *Forbes*'s list of influential Indian celebrities, and has represented India at international literature festivals in Birmingham, Sharjah and Abu Dhabi.

Her work has earned praise from major media outlets such as BBC World, *Cosmopolitan*, *The Hindu* and *The Times of India*. Preeti's accolades include the Popular Choice Fiction Award (2021), presented by *The Times of India*'s AutHER Awards, and Amazon India's Most Popular Self-Help Book of 2021. She was also named 'Indian of the Year' and received the Business Excellence Award from the New Delhi Institute of Management.

Her short stories and poems have been featured in *Condé Nast* and *Verve*. She also writes a weekly advice column and a monthly opinion column for *The Indian Express*, and has previously contributed to the *Financial Chronicle*. In addition to being a writer,

About the author

Preeti is a fitness enthusiast, an artist and a traveller. She is also a sought-after motivational speaker, having delivered talks at organizations like Walmart, Infosys, ISRO, KPMG and Accenture.

Connect with Preeti:
Website: www.preetishenoy.com
Email: ps@preetishenoy.com
Twitter/X: @Preetishenoy
Blog: Blog.preetishenoy.com
Instagram: Instagram.com/Preeti.Shenoy and Preetishenoyart
Facebook: http://preeti.io/fb
Snap: Preeti.Shenoy
LinkedIn: https://www.linkedin.com/in/preetishenoyauthor/

HarperCollins *Publishers* India

At HarperCollins India, we believe in telling the best stories and finding the widest readership for our books in every format possible. We started publishing in 1992; a great deal has changed since then, but what has remained constant is the passion with which our authors write their books, the love with which readers receive them, and the sheer joy and excitement that we as publishers feel in being a part of the publishing process.

Over the years, we've had the pleasure of publishing some of the finest writing from the subcontinent and around the world, including several award-winning titles and some of the biggest bestsellers in India's publishing history. But nothing has meant more to us than the fact that millions of people have read the books we published, and that somewhere, a book of ours might have made a difference.

As we look to the future, we go back to that one word—a word which has been a driving force for us all these years.

Read.